How to Find Meaning in Your Life
Before it Ends

· HOW TO ·

FIND

meaning

IN YOUR LIFE BEFORE IT ENDS

PATRICK RIECKE

EMERALD HOPE
PUBLISHING HOUSE

Dedication

To Kristen.

I am thankful that nearly all of the suffering in our twenty years has come from outside forces. Thank you for being... Kristen.

This book was published on our twentieth wedding anniversary, but I still feel like that kid at Johnson Bible College. The scene where I meet my sweetheart at 5:00 am under the prayer oak still plays in the top ten moments of my life.

Marrying you is the second best decision I have made in my life. As you know, Christ comes first.

Contents

Cover Credit ix

Acknowledgements x

Why This Book Is Needed xii

The Search for Meaning 1

Three Phases of Spiritual Growth 7

The Meaning of Meaning 17

How to Use the List 28

Case Study #1: Bethany's Words to Express 35

Words to Express: 34 Ways to Find
Meaning 47

Case Study #2: Robert's Actions to Take 72

Actions To Take: 33 More Ways to Find
Meaning 85

Case Study #3: George's Gifts to Provide 109

Gifts to Provide: 34 More Ways to Find Meaning   *118*

Find Meaning Every Day   *146*

The Master of Meaning and Suffering   *149*

Appendix A--A Note to Professionals   *153*

Appendix B--Advance Care Planning   *157*

More Resources   *171*

Cover Credit

Cover creation by Rebecca Koverman. Rebecca designed a cover for a friend's book. It was gorgeous. As soon as I was ready to think about a cover for this book, I wrote to my friend and asked for her contact information.

Thank you, Rebecca, for a job well done. Thank you, also, for being great to work with.

Find more of Rebecca's work at www.kovermandesign.com.

Acknowledgements

This was a group effort. I have lost track of how many friends, colleagues, and family members have read drafts of this book before publication.

Thank you to Tim O'Sullivan, Stacy Roach, Ben Miles, Chris Brinneman, Ann Jones, Kristen Riecke, Debi Binkley, Chariee Reason, and Kelly and Steve DuMond.

My saintly mother, Nancy Riecke, read the entire draft and gave notes in 36 hours. Then she worried that she had taken too long. I love you, mom. Thank you for being a dialogue partner for all my work.

Jon Swanson gave a multitude of feedback from the beginning and until the end, just like he did on *How to Talk*. I'm not very confident that I would have ever published a book if it weren't for Jon. As the icing on the cake, his bride, Nancy, has been my proofreader for both books. The quality of this book was improved exponentially because of both Swansons. Thank you.

Find Jon online at www.300wordsaday.com.

Why This Book Is Needed

The two dozen hospital chaplains in our department have each had a similar experience. A conversation begins with a stranger, and they ask a common question.

"Where do you work?"

When they hear that the chaplain works at a hospital, they ask the next logical question.

"What do you do there?"

"I am a chaplain," they respond.

"Oh, that's interesting. What does a chaplain do at the hospital?"

Most of our chaplains would like to pass on that question because there's no easy answer. What should we say? We could answer in many ways.

We respond when a sixteen-year-old has been shot. We respond when a mother has been given a terrifying diagnosis. We respond when a grandfather has a heart attack. When a grandmother has a stroke. We respond when a mom has to say goodbye to her baby, whether that baby has lived in mom's womb for just six weeks, or that "baby" is a senior citizen himself. We respond when a mom wants her (dead) baby baptized. We respond when the police are hovering around the toddler because the grieving father might actually be the perpetrator of the offense that led to this emergency room visit.

We respond when the family is singing a last hymn before removing the medical interventions that are keeping their loved one breathing. Our chaplains serve people facing these losses and more...

Every. Single. Shift. Twenty-four hours a day. Seven days a week. Three-hundred sixty-five days per year.

We know death.

We know grief.

We know pain.

If all your worst nightmares and greatest hopes were combined to create a box office movie, chaplains would be the audience in the theater. We are seldom characters in the story, but we observe, care, and support you and yours with all our hearts.

When a whole team of professionals observes this kind of pain as a part of their every workday, they have to believe there can be meaning found in suffering.

That was the point of destination at the end of my first book, *How to Talk with Sick, Dying and Grieving People: When There are No Magic Words to Say.* "Meaning can be found in suffering." To be honest, I did not intend to write this

If we didn't believe that God could help us find meaning in suffering, I suppose we would have all quit by now.

second book. Simply saying that meaning in the midst of suffering was the theme of Phase Three seemed sufficient, initially. However, one day I was speaking to a large group of professionals about the Three Phases in *How to Talk*, and I said something that was not in my notes. When I spoke about Phase Three, that meaning can be found in suffering, I said, "We've got to do better at helping people figure out *how* to find meaning in suffering."

I surprised myself with how indignant I was when I said it. Small tears formed just under my lower eyelids on both sides. My heart rate elevated, and my face flushed. It was a signal that I had something else to say. Something we all need. Something my team needs. Something I need.

This book is my necessary effort to add to the conversation about how to do just that—*how* to find meaning in suffering.

So, meaning *can* be found in suffering.

Here's how…

The Search for Meaning

I have the opportunity to lead a team of chaplains that intersect with trauma, death, and grief every day.

Essentially, the emotional foundation for this book is the sense that we have to find meaning, or we will despair.

Perhaps you have felt that way yourself.

Perhaps you feel that way for yourself or another person right now. Certainly, you can intuitively understand the need to find meaning in suffering, if such meaning can be found.

Viktor Frankl was a name I was familiar with through frequently-used quotes, but for the book in your hands now, he has been a reading companion.

Frankl writes in *Man's Search for Meaning*, 1959, "There is nothing in the world, I venture to say, that would so effectively help one to survive even the worst conditions as the knowledge that there is a meaning in one's life."[1]

Frankl knows about survival. In fact, 'survivor' is one of the primary words used to describe him.

He was a neurologist and psychiatrist but is most often noted as being a survivor of the Jewish Holocaust.

Frankl describes the extinction camps he lived in for three years as laboratories in which to study the phenomenon of finding meaning in suffering.

Before we can approach *how* we can find meaning in our suffering, we must consider three of Frankl's conclusions–conclusions we can be thankful that another soul won at great cost and has shared with us.[2]

THE POWER OF THE INNER LIFE

First, Frankl writes extensively about his continual discovery of his own inner life. He describes his inner spirit as "piercing through the enveloping gloom" of imminent death.[3]

For many, a second experience dawns upon them as they face the worst moments of their lives. While they certainly sense the "enveloping gloom", there is often the emergence, perhaps for the first time, of something inside of them they were only vaguely aware of previously.

You might call it soul, spirit, or inner life. Others might call it their "true self" or heart.

Often we find that when our normal experiences of life have faded away (like Frankl in a concentration camp or when we face our own mortality), we instead experience an abnormally direct encounter with our fundamental selves.

While many have theorized about this, Frankl witnessed it, not only in himself but in his fellow prisoners.

When we are in the midst of a health crisis, a terminal or chronic diagnosis, or already plunged into grief, it can be exceedingly difficult to see past the enveloping gloom. However, Frankl experienced the emergence of a powerful inner life.

In the chapters ahead, we will submerge ourselves in stories and tools that will help us to plumb these depths in ourselves and in those for whom we care.

MEANING CAN BE FOUND

Second, Frankl maintains that even when life seems its most meaningless, meaning does not totally elude us.

"We must never forget that we may also find meaning in life even when confronted with a hopeless situation when facing a fate that cannot be changed."[4]

Whatever painful moment you are encountering, and when the words of your friends come up empty, you can look to Frankl as a man who understood suffering. He urges you to never forget that meaning *can* be found, even in your deepest moments of suffering.

The "fate that cannot be changed" in the quote above reminds us of Phase Three from my previous book, which will be discussed in chapter one.

MEANING IS SPECIFIC AND CONCRETE

Third, Frankl argues that "questions about the meaning of life can never be answered by sweeping statements. 'Life' does not mean something vague, but something very real and concrete."[5] You already know, from the title of this book, that the coming chapters will discuss practical ways to find meaning. Meaning is sometimes viewed as philosophical and universal. However, that is not how we will view meaning in this volume. The list of 101 ways to find meaning will be practical, specific, and concrete.

Let me explain. It's not that helpful to say, "What matters is being with family." Or "Love is really what life is all about." As true and agreeable as those statements may be, when a man is huddled in his bed, despairing after his spouse has died, or a woman is bravely facing the third trimester with her baby who has a major medical disorder, such statements may fall flat. Meaning is not found in catchphrases or clichés. Meaning is person-specific. One-size does *not* fit all.

So, Frankl uncovers these three truths which will light our path in the coming chapters:

1. First, the inner life often emerges in unforeseen ways during suffering.

2. Second, meaning *can* be found in the most difficult times.

3. Third, all meaning is specific and concrete.

What are needed are real, concrete ways to find meaning, specific to the person and situation. That's what I will give you in this book. You will experience this list as a guided tour of possible ways to make meaning. The list is divided into three main parts; Words to Express, Actions to Take, and Gifts to Provide. Before each of these three parts, a case study will introduce what you will experience in that section. Then, each of the three parts will be further divided into certain themes. Within each section, a few items will be highlighted for their ease, impact, or cost.

Before I share the list with you, however, we need to lay a bit of groundwork. We need to agree on the need for meaning, its characteristics, and how we will understand those characteristics. First, how has suffering impacted your spiritual life, values, and perspective? Are you in Phase One, Phase Two, or Phase Three?

For more tools, sign up for my online course on How to Talk with Sick, Dying, and Grieving People, find meaning, prepare advance directives, talk with children about grief and so much more at PatrickRiecke.com/courses.

Notes

1. Frankl, Viktor Emil. *Man's Search for Meaning*. Beacon Press, 2006. p. 103.

2. Frankl's wife was forced to abort their first child and was, herself, subsequently murdered by Nazi soldiers in the camp where she was imprisoned. Frankl's parents also died in a separate camp. Frankl, himself, had Typhoid Fever and nearly died before his rescue.

3. Frankl, 41

4. Frankl, 112

5. Frankl, 77

Three Phases of Spiritual Growth

For us to move forward, we need to look back.

My first book, *How to Talk with Sick, Dying and Grieving People: When There are No Magic Words to Say*, was a total outpouring of my heart. That book is built around "Three Phases of Spiritual Growth" (how we change internally as we face obstacles and problems in life). In the pages ahead, I will use this framework for how we experience difficulties and how we find meaning.

PHASE ONE: GOD'S LOVE AND MY PLANS

Phase One's theme is "God loves me and has a wonderful plan for my life." This is where the story of faith usually begins. In some Christian circles, we might call this the Gospel. It is the good news we usually share with people as they enter or grow up in a community of faith. It's conventional spiritual wisdom.

The theme verse is often "'I know the plans I have for you,' declares the Lord, 'plans to prosper you and not to harm you. Plans to give you a hope and a future.'"[1]

PHASE TWO: GOD'S HELP AND MY STRUGGLES

Phase Two's theme is "God helps me overcome my difficulties and struggles," because, inevitably, we face hardships in life.

Sometimes tough times crop up immediately when we begin our spiritual journey, and Phase One and Phase Two overlap right away. Other times, we can bask in and experience God's love and favor for an extended time before the road gets too bumpy.

In Phase Two, the theme of our spiritual lives is relying on God's help and the help of those close to us to get through, past, or around our difficulties. The theme verse for Christians in this phase is Romans 8:28, "God will work all things together for the good of those who love him and are called according to his purpose." This leads to verse 37, in which we are called "more than conquerors through him who loved us."

We spend most of our lives in Phase Two, overcoming one difficulty after another. Our lives might be described as a chain of overcoming or, at least, outlasting one difficulty after another. Certainly, many books, songs, sermons, and other art have been dedicated to Phase Two, and deservedly so. These works help us along our daily journey.

But what do we call it when we will no longer overcome? How do we describe the phenomenon when we can't get past this difficulty, at least not in the way we had hoped; when we face Frankl's "fate that cannot be changed"? This unchangeable fate is more common than we would like to admit.

PHASE THREE: FINDING MEANING

Once we begin to feel as though we are not going to overcome our difficulties, finding meaning can become what matters most. Therefore, the theme of Phase Three is "God will help me find meaning in my suffering."

The theme verse for Phase Three was harder for me to discover. And, to be honest, *How To Talk* ends without a theme verse for Phase Three. Since that time, I have rediscovered a little verse in one of my favorite parts of Scripture.

The book of Ecclesiastes is one of the most depressing, ancient books. It opens with a visceral declaration that everything in life is meaningless. "Meaningless, meaningless," says the writer. "Everything is completely meaningless!"[2] In the context of words dripping with nihilistic darkness, the writer shines this ray of light:

"[God] has made everything beautiful in its time. God has also set eternity in the human heart; yet no one can fathom what God has done from beginning to end."[3]

Phase One is about *Plans.*

Phase Two is about *Help.*

Phase Three is about *Meaning.*

If you have ever sat across the table from someone who knew she was facing her own death or watched a grieving mother reach out to another hurting soul, or sat at the bedside of a dying person, you have experienced meaning in Phase Three.

What you have experienced is God making something beautiful in its time. You have experienced eternity, that unfathomable arc of what God has been doing from beginning to end.

FINDING YOUR PHASE, FINDING THEIR PHASE

If you are going to help others in their phase, you should also evaluate your phase. If you are in Phase One, with no major problems right now, and looking forward to a great future, then embrace your phase. If you are in Phase Two, finding the help you need from God or others to overcome daily battles, then fight on, and I pray you get the help you need to overcome. At the time of this writing, I am in Phase Two, with hints of Phase One and a deep appreciation for Phase Three. It's unlikely many of you reading these words are in Phase Three, but encountering Phase Three at some point(s) is unavoidable.

I have been in Phase Three, at least once. Learning that our first child had died before birth slingshotted us right past Phase Two and into Phase Three, desperately trying to find meaning in our suffering. I'll share about Stephen later.

You cannot control what phase you are in. So don't try. Just become aware of where you are.

Next, if you want to help someone else, you need to try to figure out what phase she is in. Is she just excited about what life will bring her? Talking about plans and future? Then she is probably in Phase One. Join her there and celebrate what may be coming her way and help her imagine the goodness that God is bringing her.

Is she talking about fighting and getting better, despite current obstacles? Then, she is likely in Phase Two, overcoming her obstacles. Cheer her on. Pray for her to overcome. Find ways you can help her in the midst of her struggle.

However, if only the people around her (her family and friends) are talking about overcoming and she isn't…that may be an indication that she's in a different place than the others. Is she talking about trying to understand or make sense out of her situation? Is she asking long-term questions about how her current suffering is going to impact her own life or others she cares about? If she's in Phase Three and everyone else is trying to stay in Phase Two, you have an opportunity to help her by wading into Phase Three with her. You cannot, and probably should not, try to coerce people to move from one phase to another. However, you can be a safe place for them if they are moving into Phase Three.

DEATH IS A SACRED MOMENT

The very first time I presented material on this topic, a participant approached me at a break. "Are you going to talk about how death is a sacred moment?"

Although it wasn't in my notes that day, this is a basic truth of every death—whether sudden or expected. Every person who dies is breathing one moment and the next—they are dead.

My friend Tony's moment came in a hospice facility. And it was, indeed, a sacred moment. The family had called me, feeling Tony was in his last hours.

They were right.

Back then, I didn't know that most people aren't able to interact much with those around them in the hours preceding death. Between their waning capacities, sickness, and medicine, a thick fog can be created, too thick to break through.

But when I walked into the room, Tony—a friend I had known for only a year—looked up at me and said, "Patrick!" It was the only word I heard him say in that room. And you could have knocked me over with a feather when he did.

As a pastor, I want to help people. The rest of that day, there was no real help I could offer. I sat near the family, near Tony. I don't remember if I ever prayed—though I probably did. I know that I cried and that I held Tony's hand.

Just like there are no magic words to help someone in Phase Three, there are no perfect words to describe how sacred the moment of death is. But if you have been there—you know. If you are asked to help with a funeral or memorial service, I recommend by my friend Dr. Jon Swanson's book, *Giving a Life Meaning: How to Lead Funerals, Memorial Services, and Celebrations of Life.*

Without drawing a too close comparison, the moment of death has something in common with the moment of birth. One is usually happy while the other is usually sad. But there is a sense of connection to the arc of the universe, what God is doing from beginning to end, some invisible, meaningful quality that most "normal" experiences lack.

WADING INTO PHASE THREE

I will describe the willingness to have hard conversations and do hard things for and with people in these moments of suffering as "wading" into Phase Three.

As a teenager, I once found myself walking out into an urban river near my home. The brown water obscured the muck at the bottom. With each step, my feet went deeper into the muck, which ended up reaching to my knees. A friend with me lost his shoes somewhere deep in the mud.

That's a bit what it feels like sometimes to wade into Phase Three.

You have to move slowly.

It gets deep very quickly.

It can be hard to get back out.

And you may leave part of yourself behind.

Before we can find meaning in Phase Three, we have to be *willing* to enter Phase Three.

I remember walking with a family to see their loved one who had just died. We stepped outside the consult room and toward the room in the emergency

Which is easier, to pray for someone to get better, to become healthier, or to listen to a person who believes their death is inevitable?

14

department where their loved one was alone and still. In the few dozen steps, the patient's spouse looked at me with a ghastly expression.

"This is your job?" she gaped. "Just being with people when other people die?"

"Yes ma'am. It really is an honor." I replied.

Her eyes widened as she threw her head to the side, trying to take in the scene.

"I could never do that," she exhaled just before we reached the heavy wooden door, which, when opened, would reveal the most important person in her life, dead and lifeless.

Many have noticed that our culture has become more superficial as time goes on. I am unsure if that is true. However, I am sure that many people are uncomfortable in Phase Three moments.

That's why we need help.

And helpers.

And more books like this one.

And people like you.

Phase Three is a frightening, serene, and important place.

Meaning can be found, but what do we mean by "meaning"?

Notes

1. Jeremiah 29:11, NIV
2. Ecclesiastes 1:2
3. Ecclesiastes 3:11

The Meaning of Meaning

Of course, before we go further in our consideration of how to find meaning in suffering, we must decide how we will define such a commonly-used word as *meaning*.

Melissa Kelley, in her book on grief theory, admits, "Despite such common uses, the meaning of *meaning* is often vague or fuzzy."[1] In light of this modern fuzziness about what meaning is, we remember Frankl's insistence that meaning is specific and concrete. With a lack of clarity on what meaning *means,* we will take a simple approach to a definition. We will consider just two qualities of what gives meaning to words, actions, and gifts. But first, let me tell you about a time when my heart broke under a meaningful weight.

WHEN A FEATHER WEIGHS A TON

One day a chaplain called me in my office. She was in our Family Birthing Center. She said we had a situation. Now, the chaplains have situations daily. Sometimes hourly. For an incomplete list, from traumas to notaries, reread the preface of this book. So, when the chaplain told me she had a situation, I knew she meant that she had run into something above and beyond the "normal" death, trauma, and pain that we usually encounter.

She had run into something above and beyond the "normal" death, trauma, and pain that we usually encounter.

She asked if I could come down right away, which I did. When I arrived, she was standing near the large nursing module at the bend in the hall. She led me to a post-partum room. Inside the room was a tiny baby. The tiny baby was no longer alive. That's a situation, but one that the chaplain typically could have handled without support.

What made this a 'situation' was one person who was absent from the room. Dad was there. Grandparents were there, and a smattering of aunts, uncles, and others, but not mom.

"Mom is in the ICU [Intensive Care Unit]." The chaplain explained.

Mom had been in a traumatic motor vehicle crash. The crash was bad enough to end the life of the fragile baby in her uterus, even though surgeons acted quickly. It was also bad enough to land mom in ICU.

She was unresponsive. She had not yet been able to know. To know that her baby had died.

"They have a question that I could not answer." Our chaplain began. The room was heavy with salty tears and momentariness.

"They want to know if the baby can go to ICU to visit Mom. They know she won't be awake, but they wonder if they can take pictures of the two of them together. This might be their only chance." She knew that I didn't have a canned answer for this situation but trusted that we would find a way to help find meaning in the midst of incredible suffering.

I paused.

Not because I needed to assess my willingness, the willingness of the nurses on either unit or any questions of liability. I know the heart of my health system, and it's not the sort of place where I would get in any trouble for honoring this family's request–if at all possible.

I paused because the walk from one unit to the other is long. And mostly in public spaces. I tried to envision the best possible route to honor the baby–not wanting to unnecessarily expose him to public view. I tried to envision the best possible route to honor the dad–knowing he would be making the hardest walk of his life. I tried to consider respect for the rest of our hospital, often crowded with people in the midst of their own stories.

I looked to my unlikely partner for the painful undertaking before us. Security officer Larry. Officer Larry knows how to transport patients after they have died. Larry also knows how to get around the hospital. With a plan in place, dad scooped up his child, and we exited the room.

Officer Larry and I led a small and painful parade through the hallways on a long walk from the Family Birthing Center to the ICU. Nurses honored this little life with a hush. And accommodations.

We took pictures.

We prayed and cried.

Eventually, dad needed to leave. Grandma asked, "How will we get the baby back to his room?"

Our chaplain with the beautiful soul spoke up. "My boss and Officer Larry can help with that. Don't you worry."

And so it was that I found myself, escorted by Officer Larry, traversing a half-mile of hallways with a dead baby in my arms.

He probably only weighed a pound.

But he weighed a ton.

Because baby loss is such a painful topic, my wife, Kristen, and I have written an entire book on the topic. *No Matter How Small: Understanding Miscarriage and Stillbirth* provides you with heartrending stories of loss, but also practical tools to understand and cope with this special pain.

THE MEANING OF MEANING

In the introduction, we recalled Viktor Frankl's teaching in *Man's Search for Meaning*. Meaning is individual and specific. That doesn't mean there isn't some use in trying to define, generally, what meaning actually is. It does mean that a universal description of the concept of meaning will always be lacking.

For our purposes, let's consider meaning as having **two primary characteristics.**

First, meaning has *weight*–in the way that ordering your lunch at a restaurant does not seem to have weight, but going to a job interview, or wedding, does.

Some universal agreement on what has moral and emotional weight can be found. Birth, life, death, and relationships all have weight. And they have weight and meaning in many contexts, in many cultures, and probably throughout all of time.

21

However, beyond that universal agreement, many actions, moments, items, and words have meaning to some but not others.

But weight is something that is felt.

When have you felt the weight of meaning? The birth of a child? The completion of a degree?

What about the smaller moments that you felt had meaning?

The first primary characteristic of meaning is *weight*. It doesn't have to weigh as much as a tiny baby, but it does have to weigh more than selecting your clothes on any given day.

A CONVERSATION DECADES IN THE MAKING

Emily Esfahani Smith, in exploring the "four pillars of meaning", finds the third to be transcendence.[2] Transcendence is the sense that we are connected with something bigger (and longer) than our own lives.[3] Kelley also suggests that finding our place within a narrative, a greater story helps those in grief to make meaning.

Finding meaning often means discovering how today's situation connects with either the past or the future.

Speaker and author Simon Sinek, in a presentation on leadership, said it this way. "What does it mean to live an infinite life? Our lives are finite. But life itself is infinite. We will literally live forever because of the impact we make on those around us."[4]

After I started working as a chaplain, I had many conversations with my leader.[5] One, in particular, had a sense of connection to a much larger story.

We were standing in her office when she asked me, "So, how are you related to Gladys Riecke?"

She tilted her head back to look at my face through her reading glasses.

"She's my grandmother," I replied. I was thinking, "She's been dead for more than two decades. I can't remember the last time someone asked me about her." My grandmother was born more than a century before the conversation in the chaplaincy office.

"I thought so," she spoke slowly. "When I was a young mother, struggling to get my three squirmy children to hold still during church service, a woman at church became my mentor. She sought me out weekly to encourage me, telling me about bringing six children, a daughter, and five sons, with her to church for many years, even though her husband had died before the oldest child was an adult. She understood. And she cared about me. That woman—was your grandmother."

In a flash, I felt connected to a story that began before I was born and, perhaps, would continue even after I die.

I encountered the second characteristic of meaning: *permanence.*

Permanence is the sense that something will not end even if my life comes to an end. If that story about my leader and my grandmother doesn't have actual permanence, at least it has the sense that it extends past the boundaries of my own life.

Finding meaning often means finding how today's situation connects either with the past or the future.

One of the greatest pains of death is that it is the end of us. Or at least it feels that way. And if I am over, at least on this earth, does my meaning go away as well? And if my meaning goes away at the time of death, do I even really have any significance now? If I can do something now that will live beyond my own life, then I have a sense of being eternal, being at least a shade more permanent than my actual life is.

Therefore, for our purposes, we will consider meaning as having these two qualities:

1. **Weight,** like a tiny baby in your arms

2. **Permanence,** when you can see how today connects with the past and/or future

Every item on the upcoming list, whether words to express, actions to take, or gifts to provide, have either one or both of these two qualities–weight and permanence.

WHY "FIND"?

Finally, I purposefully talk about finding meaning in suffering, because I believe meaning always exists in every circumstance. I do not believe that meaning is something we have to create or make. Therefore, I have not spoken about making meaning. I also believe that many times, the existential meaning in a job, situation, life, painful moment is not apparent. It can be obvious, but more often it is hidden. At times like this, the meaning must be "found", much like one finds words in a puzzle, or finds an unexpected treasure, one can 'find' meaning.

It's similar to an experience I have regularly. Having four children, I often hear the audio of an electronic device without seeing the picture on the screen. Perhaps they are watching a video on one of their devices across the family room, or in the backseat of our vehicle while I am driving.

When all I hear is the noise, it's usually irritating. It's especially irritating when the video loops and plays several times in a row.

This can be how we feel about pain and suffering in our lives.

We hear the noise, and it's irritating. If it goes on for some time, feeling as though it's looping repetitively, it becomes all the more frustrating.

However, if my children and I are at the kitchen table and my son is watching a video whose sound I hear, I have an opportunity.

I can stand up, circle the table, and view the picture that accompanies the audio. Often I have done this with my children. A video has played several times and the audio is grating at my nerves. Chances are, I am not able to make sense of the sound without the advantage of seeing the visual.

But then I circle the table and begin to view the picture along with the sound.

And it's a hilarious video.

A touching segment.

Or maybe it's still irritating, but at least the audio makes some sense to me now.

When we are going through painful times, we may be inclined to only hear the noise, and the noise certainly is irritating, especially if it seems to be looping over and over and over...

But when we circle the table and view the picture as well, we *find meaning,*

That doesn't mean we will like the video. The video may be unpleasant, frustrating, or sad. But finding the meaning of the noise can help. We haven't created meaning. But we have found it.

Therefore, we will talk about *finding* meaning, experiences that have a sense of *weight,* and *permanence.*

Notes

1. Kelley, Melissa M. *Grief: Contemporary Theory and the Practice of Ministry.* Fortress Press, 2010. p.75

2. https://www.ted.com/talks/. Search: "Emily Esfahani Smith".

3. The other pillars of belonging, purpose, and storytelling are also worth noting.

4. Global Leadership Summit, August 10, 2018

5. For a practical tool about how to visit people in the hospital, go to PatrickRiecke.com/resources for your FREE Wallet Card full of hospital visit tips.

How to Use the List

Chances are, you have never used the word "bequest". Maybe you've never heard of it. But you will find the idea of giving bequests to be quite contagious.

A bequest is a purposeful and thoughtful gift. It comes from Middle English–the thirteenth century. It's one of those words which, when you get to know it a little better, you wish was used more often today. It's connected to the word "Bequeath". Bequeath is a verb. Bequest is a noun. It can be defined as a legacy (but good luck adequately defining "legacy"). A bequest is sometimes given in a will from one generation to the next or one individual to another.

One description of a bequest begins to correlate with what we will discover in the coming pages. A bequest is something transmitted from the past to the present or future.

Viktor Frankl, in the context of the concentration camp, describes the loss of a sense of future that could sometimes befall a prisoner. Once the prisoner gave up hope on something to look forward to, he often succumbed quickly to his illness and frailty and died shortly thereafter.

When we, in modern society, experience suffering, we can feel as though we have no sense of future. We can feel as though the end of our lives is the end of us. This can occur whether or not we have a religious belief in life after death.

What if I told you that what follows is a list of words, actions, and gifts that will fill your life with meaning?

After all, even if I believe I will find an eternal paradise after I die, I will still be dead in this world, and therefore I have no future in this world.

Many people who are facing death, imminently or conceptually, find themselves terrorized by the thought of the finality of death, and life begins to lose its meaning. Once meaning is gone, strength soon follows. And when your strength is gone, joy, peace, and even love can ebb away as well.

But what if I told you that what follows is a long and practical list of bequests? What if I told you that what follows is a long and practical list of things that you can say, provide, or do, that will fill life with more meaning than you have ever experienced?

What if you could line up conversations, experiences, and gifts that will not only bring you purpose as you face suffering but will also give you a sense of future—even past your death in this world?

THE ORIGIN OF THE LIST

This list came out of a desperate sense of necessity. When your occupation includes conversations and tasks that are tinged by suicide victims, moms who miscarried this morning, or the toll road's latest victim from a dramatic motor vehicle crash, you have two choices.

One, you can despair. Then self-medicate. But you will likely give up all hope and eventually quit.

Or, you can begin to believe that, instead of sucking the meaning out of the world like a syringe, these traumatic experiences might be the open windows that let in the light of meaning.

Melissa Kelley, referencing another religious philosopher, argues that these Phase Three moments "compel us to encounter our own limitations in the face of inexorable life forces."[1] Times of trauma, pain, or grief compel us to consider our life's ultimate meaning.

+++

A hospital is a strange place.[2] One day was stranger than many others.

As the leader of our department, I no longer respond personally to a room when a patient dies. However, when a toddler dies, and it's sudden and unexplained, all my emails and meetings can be put on hold.

The chaplain who was on duty didn't need my help. He is as capable as I am at everything from the paperwork to the relational connections.

But *I* needed to go.

When I walked into that room, put my hand on dad's shoulder as he held his lifeless, perfect, round-faced, baby boy, and wrapped my arms around a mom who was coming apart at the seams, I realized the room was big enough for two chaplains.

Hours passed, and as I walked back to the office, I cut through a back hallway that passes through our oncology unit. About halfway through the unit, I could hear music coming from one hospital room. I could tell it was not recorded but live music.

Then it dawned on me.

Our Catholic priest-chaplain sings opera. (By the way, just that one sentence was worth the price you paid for this book.) And he leads a quartet of young people who sing beautiful sacred music to our patients–one at a time, in their rooms.

I paused outside the room, my mind and heart still in pieces for this family I had been with all morning–a family who would never be the same–and I eavesdropped on the pitch-perfect song of our priest's quartet. The lyrics were in Latin. The occupant, into whose room they were crowded, speaks Spanish, and was facing a scary hospitalization.

As their concert concluded, the priest blessed the patient. The quartet smiled and thanked the patient for the opportunity. They exited to the hall where I stood.

I shook each of their hands and thanked them for what they were doing.

Down the hall from the precious, dead toddler, sacred music was being perfectly performed for an audience of one person.

Many times I have said, "There ought to be a resource, a list of sorts, of things people could *do* to find meaning while they are suffering."

I believe agony and beauty live enmeshed more often than we realize. Suffering and meaning are often conjoined twins. We get to see that. I want the rest of the world to see it, too.

Suffering and meaning are often conjoined twins.

That is why I say that I have compiled the following list out of a sense of necessity.

May you find it to be beautiful music, composed for a very small audience in the midst of potentially the greatest heartbreak in your life or the life of a dear friend.

The list that follows is broken down into three main categories.

1. Words to Express

2. Actions to Take

3. Gifts to Provide

Each category has its own categories. And before each main category, you will encounter a case study that will illustrate how these words, actions, or gifts can help you find meaning

33

in suffering. In each section, I have highlighted a few items that I would like to see more people choose. So, if you aren't sure where to start, select one of the recommended items.

I hope you feel a gentle sense of anticipation and joy as we prepare to wade into Phase Three, finding meaning in suffering.

Let me begin by introducing you to a good friend. I think you'll like Bethany.

Notes

1. Kelley, 91
2. For a free practical tool to help you when you visit a hospital, go to PatrickRiecke.com/resources. A free wallet card will be mailed to you.

Case Study #1: Bethany's Words to Express

Bethany has been a part of your place of worship since she was a child. Her dad is one of the leaders at church. You've known this family for a long time.

Although Bethany is a little younger than you, the two of you have been good friends for many years.

Bethany met Brad in college and they were married shortly after graduation. Now they have three children; Haley, a middle school daughter, Micah, a son in elementary school, and Emma is their baby girl.

During Bethany's pregnancy with Emma, a regular ultrasound showed that the baby was fine. However, there was a concern for Bethany. After Emma was born, screening was done that showed a mass on one of Bethany's ovaries. After some more testing, your phone rang. It was Bethany's dad.

You could tell he had been crying. What he said next confirmed your fears.

"It's cancer." He said. "Stage three, near stage four. We need to get everyone praying. We need a miracle."

At first, Bethany struggled. Surgery, radiation, then chemotherapy.

Her cancer was aggressive, but her dad said she's a fighter, and he was right. The prayers were flying up to heaven. The church rallied around the family, bringing meals, sending notes, watching the kids, and checking in with them frequently. After all her treatments, Bethany was much weaker, but she was said to be in remission.

Several months later, however, Bethany's dad called you again.

"The cancer is back," he said. Treatments began right away. At the end of that round of treatments, though still treating her aggressively, the doctors gave her a less optimistic outlook.

Your phone rings again.

This time it's Bethany.

Although her voice is thin, her spirit is strong. She asks if she can meet with you. You rearrange your schedule for that very afternoon.

When Bethany sits down across from you, you remember her as a young girl in your church. She has always been full of life and a joy to her parents, friends, and others at the church. You remember one year when she had the lead role in a children's play. She sang a sweet little song that brought you to tears. You remember her very much at Phase One of her spiritual life—accepting the news that God loves her and has a wonderful plan for her life.

You think of her dad and mom.

Although many people seem to primarily sympathize with Bethany herself, or Brad, or the kids, you keep thinking about Bethany's parents. You have always had so much respect for them, and they have always seemed like such strong people.

Bethany's sickness has broken their hearts.

You can't help but put yourself in their shoes and think about how it must feel to helplessly watch your daughter, the mother of your precious grandchildren, face such a significant struggle. They are in Phase Two—asking God to help them overcome their difficulties.

As Bethany sits down across from you, you realize that it might be the first time you have talked with her by herself, without the rest of the crowd around. Her gaze is serious and piercing. Her body may have changed, but her engaging presence has only become more focused.

The conversation is different this time. Bethany has arrived in Phase Three. You swallow hard, sensing what is coming. After brief small talk, Bethany sits up straight in her seat.

"I know I am going to die."

She sips warm coffee and peers over the edge of the cup. She seems to be allowing you a moment to absorb what she has just said.

"I know I am going to die."

"I know my three kids are going to lose their mom before any of them reach adulthood." Small tears form in the corners of her eyes. "I'm sad for Haley and Micah. They will remember me, and I generally think that's a good thing. But Emma won't even remember me, at least not like Haley and Micah. Sometimes, that keeps me up at night."

Now you take a sip of your drink, hoping it can warm your hands and face because they have gone cold. Bethany pauses, gathers her strength after the trembling that surfaced when she said Emma's name.

She continues.

"I know Brad is going to be a widower before he even reaches middle age. He's been so supportive, and now…" Her voice trails, and so does her gaze.

Then she says the phrase that brings tears to your eyes. "My parents."

Their faces come into your mind.

You both pick up napkins from the table. Then she shares the reason she called you today.

"I had a dream last night that they were standing at the front of the church. They were dressed like it was Sunday morning, but it wasn't. They were both crying. My dad's arm was around my mom."

Her large brown eyes brim as she puts her hands on the table, her fingers on the tabletop, and her thumbs under it. Like she is steadying herself. She looks at you and says, "They were standing in front of my casket."

Her tears tumble.

Your tears tumble.

You simply wait for the moment to be complete.

Later, you won't be sure how you thought to ask this next question, but it bubbles up out of you.

"What do you want to do?" you ask, hoping that's not the stupidest thing someone could say at this moment.

Bethany does not look at you. She looks at her hands in her lap. You can tell she is deep in thought and she seems to be rallying supernatural courage. Cancer may have taken most of her physical strength, but her inner strength seems to have only grown.

After what seems like a long time, her head stays down, but her eyes turn up to you.

"I like to write." She almost grins with the anticipation of what she is about to do.

"Could I..." she probes you to see if you think she is crazy. Her head tilts.

"Could I write letters to people and then give them to you to hold on to until..." You know that she means until she dies, but you won't make her say it out loud.

A couple of tears bubble up again, but they are not altogether sad this time. There is a little bit of excitement mixed in this time as you nod your head while she tells you the rest of her plan.

+++

Bethany was right.

Seven weeks after your talk she died surrounded by love. Brad was lying in the bed next to her, holding her close, his tears blessing his bride. Their three children, including Emma, the toddler, slept in their beds. Bethany's mom and dad kept vigil in the family room.

When you woke up to the news of her death the next morning, you walked into your kitchen and stood about six feet away from the counter where a stack of envelopes laid. For what seemed like a long time, you stared at this precious pile of paper.

After lots of hugs, calls, and preparations, Bethany's funeral service draws a large crowd. As you get out of your car in the parking lot, you have a special secret.

From your passenger seat, you pick up two dozen letters in a small box—all by the same author.

Although the box only weighs a couple of pounds, it feels heavy to you. Your friend's letters have lived with you for the last couple of weeks. You aren't sure if they have been haunting you or blessing you, but their presence in your home has been palpable.

On the way to the funeral, you carefully tuck the box under your arm. Each envelope has a single name handwritten on the outside. They are sealed, and you have not seen what is inside any of them.

"What's this?" Brad asks as you hand him a thick envelope with his name on it.

You hadn't even considered that he might ask this question.

Choking back a world of emotion, you touch the sleeve of Brad's charcoal suit coat and look into his eyes.

"It's from Bethany," you say before your composure is compromised.

Brad still looks young to you, and his weary face now goes white.

"Oh my God," is all he can say. You remember when he first held Haley in his arms fifteen years ago. Now, he holds Bethany's letter with a similar look of awe on his face.

Haley finishes a conversation with a friend and comes up beside her dad.

Looking at his expression, she asks what's going on.

"What's that?" she asks, looking at her dad's letter. "It looks like mom's handwriting. But it can't…"

When she turns to look at you, your outstretched hand holds another envelope. It's nearly as thick as her dad's.

On the top is scrawled the name 'Haley'.

Always the intuitive one of the children, she knows immediately what this is. She claps her hand over her mouth and sinks her head into your left shoulder.

Two more envelopes have the names "Micah" and "Emma". Micah just says, "Cool" and stuffs it in his pocket. Emma will get hers when she is older. Bethany's mom and dad helped Bethany a bit, so they are not as surprised as others. Still, they realize how special this is.

"Thank you," says her dad. "You know, after she met with you a couple of months ago, she called me. She told me she was going to start doing this. At first, I wasn't too excited because I felt like it meant the end of her life was getting close. But, here we are."

He glances towards Bethany, in a simple white dress. She is thin but lovely in her casket. He continues, "You helped her to give a gift to us that will live with us forever." He holds up his envelope. "Thank you for being willing to have that conversation with Bethany when we couldn't."

He puts his arm around his wife, and they step over to Bethany, putting their hands on hers.

In a sudden flash, you remember your friend's dream of this very scene. It's the reason you had coffee with Bethany that afternoon.

43

Bethany dreamed about seeing her parents at church, wearing Sunday clothes, standing at her casket. You realize it was that dream that prompted her to start writing letters, and now here she is. And here they are. Time seems to stand still as you admire the trio.

After handing out several other envelopes with similar reactions, the funeral service is underway when the pastor motions for you to come to the front.

One envelope is still in the box.

It has your name on it, but it's not just for you.

Bethany asked you not to read it until her funeral. You pull it out of the box and stand to your feet.

You slowly, reverently, open the letter. Bethany had wonderful handwriting. Even as she grew weaker, it was still beautiful. You begin to read.

Friends,

When I was young, I always dreamed of having the life I had before I was diagnosed. I won't say that every day was perfect, but now I realize how fortunate I was—how fortunate I am. I believed in God's purposes for my life pretty easily. I could feel his love wrap around me like a warm blanket.

Even when I was first diagnosed, it seemed impossible that I would die from this cancer. After all, I was young and strong. How often I recalled the lessons I learned as a child. For a long time, I simply knew God would help me get through this. I prayed every day that I would be healthy again. And I know that many of you prayed that prayer with me. So many people visited, called, wrote notes, brought meals, and helped us during the past few years.

I came to a point after my second round of treatment where I could see the handwriting on the wall. I was growing weaker and the looks on the faces of my doctors began to tell me that it was unlikely I was going to recover long term. When I looked into the faces of my children, I felt so sad. When I wasn't sad, I was angry. In my mind, if God really loved me, he should help me get better.

After God tolerated all my yelling at him, the people close to us continued to pray and continued to love us. I realized that even though God wasn't fixing my problem, that God was still loving me. He was loving me through all of you.

While I would not wish cancer on any one of you, there have been gifts along this road that I treasure. I was able to tell everyone close to me how much I love them. I was able to experience grace and love every day, even when I didn't want it.

During one of the most difficult, but most important, conversations of my life, a special friend encouraged me to write letters. Many of you today have those letters in your hands. Please know that every page is anointed with my love and tears.

While I would change the story in a heartbeat so that Brad and the kids wouldn't have to go on without me, I feel closer to God and all of you because of what I have been through. I would have preferred to avoid suffering like this. But, God has been good to me, even in my suffering. For that, I am thankful.

I love you all.

Bethany[1]

Notes

1. For more of Bethany's story and her impact on those around her, read *No Matter How Small: Understanding Miscarriage and Stillbirth*

Words to Express: 34 Ways to Find Meaning

WORDS TO EXPRESS

When you are facing the end of your own life or helping a friend who might be newly diagnosed with a terminal or chronic disease, you can sense that there are words that need to be expressed. Of course, for a long time the notion that the last words that a person utters have been viewed as something significant. However, in today's medically-advanced society, we are more often incapable of communication as our life nears its end. Whether we are intubated (have a tube in our airway) in the Intensive Care Unit, sedated, or simply on a large amount of pain medication after a long medical situation, we seldom get to purposefully utter our last words moments before our last breath.

However, that doesn't mean we don't have something to say.

We just need to say it a bit sooner.

We may need to say something to another person.

We may need to say something to ourselves.

We may need to say something to God.

We may just need to say something out loud just to say it. We may need to write something down just to get it out. We may need to say something repetitively so we can come to terms with it.

Formally or informally, finding a way to express some important words can be a pathway to finding meaning in suffering.

For Bethany, she found meaning in suffering by expressing her words in letters to her loved ones, so that's where we will start.

My Top Five Picks are highlighted. I have called your attention to them because I believe that anyone could say these words, and they can make an impact in many situations.

THE WRITTEN WORD

1. Letters to Loved Ones
^Top Five Pick!^

Perhaps, like Bethany, you or the person you care about has always been better at expressing themselves through the written word than in conversation. Or, perhaps writing is preferable, because it is more durable than the spoken word. Maybe you feel like you can say *exactly* what you want to say if you write it.

Start by making a **list** of people who need to receive a letter from you. Think of it this way. *If I died tonight, would I have regrets if I didn't write a letter to this person?* If you don't feel you may have a sense of regret, maybe you don't need to write anything to that person.

Once you have your list, decide on your **method** of recording.

Can someone scribe your letters for you?
Is it important that you handwrite them?
Would it be better for you to type your words?
Is there a simple piece of technology that would assist you in putting these letters together in the timeframe you desire?

Lastly, choose a **delivery** method.

How will these be given?
When will they be delivered? Before your death or after? At your funeral?
Will they be given privately or publicly?
Will they be carried to the recipients by a trusted person?

When we are seeking to find meaning in suffering, we are essentially seeking to find ways that our true self will live on and be connected to what matters to us even after we have died–we are seeking permanence. Writing letters to loved ones can be a powerful way to find meaning.

2. Letters on Special Days

As a variation of #1, consider writing multiple letters to your closest loved ones that are intended for special days. Here are just a few occasions to consider:

- A child's wedding
- Your wedding anniversary
- A graduation
- A baptism or confirmation
- The birth of a grandchild
- A child or friend's first house, child, job, or other accomplishments

Think of the days in the future that you look forward to yourself, and think of the days you will regret missing if you cannot be there. Those are the special days for which you should write letters now.

3. Blog—public or secret

Blogging, or something similar, is so accessible that you almost need a reason *not* to do this.

You could use this simply as a platform for many of the other items on this list. Develop your own goal and get blogging!

CONVERSATIONS TO HAVE

4. Making Peace
^Top Five Pick!^

Having a longstanding (or relatively new) conflict with someone in our lives can be like a burr under a saddle. It can chafe and cause a constant low level of pain and frustration.

One day a chaplain was visiting a patient who was near the end of his life. During their conversation, the patient mentioned a son that he had not talked with in months. Something had happened, and they had a falling out. The hospitalized man was confident that his son would not be coming to see him.

Probing just a bit, our chaplain asked, "Do you want him to come to see you?"

The man paused and was silent for a long time. That's not unusual for someone in the hospital. Between the pain, sickness, and medication, sometimes we need to wait patiently.

Our chaplain finished the story with tears in his own eyes. "As I sat there watching his face, I saw one tear roll down. Then another. Then I noticed that he was staring at his phone in his hands. I could guess what he was thinking. Finally, he looked up at me through many tears and said. 'Yes. Yes, I would like it if he would come to see me.'"

Before the chaplain could exit the room, this patient was on the phone with his son.

Chances are, if you need to make amends with someone, you don't need to think about it too long. The hard part is not figuring out if you conflict with someone. The hard part is admitting it, calling that person, or writing out the words you need to say.

For a person in Phase Three, in a moment of struggle that isn't going to be easily overcome, meaning can be found by making peace with loved ones; and that peace can extend your presence in positive ways even after your death.

Is there anyone with whom you are at odds and is causing you pain?

5. The Three Words

For years, when interviewing chaplain applicants, I have asked this question. "If you had to describe yourself in three words, what would they be?"

I've heard everything from 'funny' to 'faithful'. Usually, I ask them to expand on one of the three words, and the stories they tell and the circumstances they describe are very revealing.

What three words would best describe you?

6. How I came to faith

A friend's dad was dying a few years ago. We thought he was going to die quickly, in his first hospitalization. Thankfully, he did not. But he was far from healthy and was certainly in Phase Three–attempting to find meaning in suffering.

During that time we attended a silent auction fundraiser for an organization we care about. There were many interesting items on which we bid that night. But one, in particular, caught my wife Kristen's eye and made her think of our friend, Bre, and her dad, Mike.

A retired English teacher was offering to interview a person and write their testimony–the story of how they came to embrace their Christian faith.

Kristen bid on it and won. A few weeks later this dear woman arrived at Mike's apartment with a list of questions and a notepad and pen. She spent a couple of hours interviewing Mike that afternoon.

Later, Mike and Bre received a copy of Mike's testimony, compiled professionally by this English teacher. Mike's life lives on in this book.

You don't need a silent auction or a professional writer. A person willing to listen and write down what you tell them would suffice if you cannot do it on your own.

COMPLETE THIS SENTENCE

7. "If I would have had more time, I would have…"

Tell your loved ones what you would have done if you would have lived, healthy, for ten more years, or fifty more.

Would you have learned Portuguese and moved to Brazil?

Would you have written poems?

Would you have become a yoga instructor?

Speaking these dreams out loud or writing them down can do three things:

1. Help you grieve what you didn't get to do
2. Help you feel like you have expressed your desires
3. Inspire someone else to do those very things

8. "When I was young I always wanted to…"

The goal here isn't to think through your regrets and inspire others to do those things. The goal here is to share a little bit about what you were like when you were younger. Did you have dreams of being a great singer, so you drove everyone crazy singing all the time?

My family loves a story I tell about when I was in first grade.

Having told my parents I wanted to be a priest when I grew up, I was the pride of the family (this was short-lived, and you are about to learn why).

At a wedding reception, we sat with the priest who had performed the wedding mass. Apparently, I was pretty interested in a little girl at the next table who was about my age.

The priest leaned across the table, knowing I had expressed a premature interest in the priesthood, and said to the precocious boy sitting in his Sunday best, "You know, Patrick, if you are going to be a priest, you are going to have to stop making eyes at the ladies."

My gaze snapped from the little girl to the priest. I said nothing. However, I gave up my dreams of being a priest right then and there.

My desire to be a priest as a young child, while not realized, tells others something about me. A way of thinking about me that lives on even if I am sick, dying, or already gone.

And my interest in being in a meaningful relationship with a woman (though immature in this story) is reflected in my loving marriage to Kristen.

What did you want to do when you were eight years old? When you were thirteen, or when you finished school? Those dreams are an important part of you that can continue to live on for generations to come.

9. "If I could relive one day over and over, it would be..."

Would you relive the day you came to faith in God? The day you went to the amusement park with your best friend? The day you were married? The day you got an award or job?

Telling this anecdote about yourself to someone, or even just saying it out loud, can help us find meaning. We feel the weight of that memory, and it gives us a sense of permanence.

10. "If I could change one thing about my life, it would be..."

Finishing this sentence doesn't need to be filled with regret. If you have people to make peace with, and the conflict hurts your heart, you can go back up to #4 in this chapter.

Would you have been a different religion from childhood? Taken that job in that faraway city? Not wasted time worrying about your finances?

11. "After I am dead, please don't..."

One of my favorite ways to complete this sentence has been "don't make me a saint." The person who expressed this fear of canonization was all too aware that in a eulogy, at a funeral, in the newspaper and online, even in personal conversations, the living avoid speaking ill of the dead. That's respectable, of course, but sometimes that leads to talking about the person like he was a pasty-faced nun who did no wrong, cared for the needy, and routinely gave up his possessions. While that would be admirable, it would not be interesting (or honest).

I've told Kristen that I do not want the twenty-third Psalm read at my funeral ("The Lord is my shepherd, I shall not want...").[1] That's not because I have anything against that scripture passage. Rather, it is because I have heard it or read it myself at so many funerals, it feels trite and lacks meaning for me.

What is your fear after you die? Whether it's relational like the person who did not want to be a saint, or specific and practical like my refusal of Psalm 23, it's acceptable for you to tell people. It might be funny, and will definitely be specific to you.

12. "The thing that makes me the maddest is..."

Our passions are often discovered in our anger. Is there a politician or political issue that makes you mad? Why does it make you mad? What does that say about what's inside of you?

My mother advocated for the inclusion of women in an all men's service group when I was young. Her strength at standing up to the status quo inspired me.

That inspiration was born in anger.

"We're the ones doing all the work, anyways." She would argue. "We're good enough to do the work, but not good enough to be members? That's not right."

I carry my mother's passion for equality (displayed in her anger) with me in my ministry today.

13. "My faith increased or was tested when..."

We've all had stretching experiences that have altered how we view the world, how we view God, scripture, or the community of faith.

When did you experience watershed moments that increased your faith?

That could be meaningful to tell someone.

14. "If I had to waste an afternoon, I would..."

How we spend free time often reveals our specific inner selves. Would you read, call a friend, or play a sport?

If you would go golfing, and your niece loves to golf, she might feel connected to you (and thereby to something greater than herself–an experience of permanence) every time she hits the links. But if she doesn't know, an opportunity to find meaning may be lost.

15. "If I could tell my 20-year-old-self three things, they would be..."

While this offers reminiscence, like #8, it also gives you a free pass to advise the younger generation.

16. "My favorite meal includes (Entrée, appetizer, side, drink, and dessert)..."

Kate was a special baby. I didn't get to meet her, she died before she was two-years-old, but I am glad we eventually met Kate's family. Our children are friends and we treasure this family.

Krista and Andy and their boys started a non-profit in Kate's name. Kate's Kart[2] brings new books to hospitalized children. Because Kate loved books.

But she also loved ice cream.

Now, Kate's Kart hosts a huge ice cream social for our community each year (it's one-half festival, one-half fundraiser). Additionally, dozens of families (including my own) have ice cream on Kate's birthday and post the pictures online.

Identifying and discussing favorite foods has more meaning than we might think.

17. "My favorite snack is…"
^Top Five Pick!^

Snacks carry an emotional quotient that's different from meals.

Friends of my children love to give them candy and treats as gifts for their birthdays. It means, "I noticed you like this, and by giving it to you, I feel connected to you."

When we share this with our loved ones, it opens up the opportunity for them to feel connected to us every time they enjoy that snack.

18. "The career I secretly wish I would have pursued is…."

Did you always think you would have made a great nurse? Racecar driver? One way to express yourself to those who care about you and might follow in your footsteps is to tell them what career you realize, in retrospect, might have been a perfect fit for you.

19. "My favorite holiday is…"

And why?

PRACTICALLY SPEAKING

20. Develop Your Will Thoughtfully

This is not legal advice, but compose your will thoughtfully, with more than just "Jimmy gets the dishes." Instead, maybe you can say, "Jimmy gets the dishes because of his hospitable heart. I always loved having meals at his house."

A financial planner or attorney will help you with the specifics of the will, but that doesn't mean you can't include your personality and add weight and permanence to the simple items you leave behind.[3]

21. Consider Life Insurance Money

If you have life insurance, have some conversations with the beneficiaries. You don't have to dictate what they will do, that might be a negative example of adding weight and permanence. But a conversation about ideas will help them feel like you are more present with them once you are gone.

22. Pre-plan Your Funeral, Grave Site, and Headstone

Will your headstone be spiritual, meaningful, funny, or simple? That message could be impactful for many generations to come, so talk with people about where you will be buried, and find out what is meaningful to them. Talk about what you do and don't want at your funeral.[4]

23. Your Birthday

When you are gone (and we will all be gone one day), your birthday could be a hollow time for those who are still living. That day can also be a time when they might feel a little lost. Do I go to work on the birthday of my dead loved one? It's a little hard to explain to my boss why I need that day off.

Maybe you could give them your thoughts on what to do on your birthday. Watch a funny or sad show. Eat something you like. Go to your favorite places.

They don't have to follow through on your wishes, but knowing your wishes might give them a little direction on a day that can feel disorienting.

24. Anniversary of your death

Talk about what others can do on the anniversary of your death.

More thoughts on this at the end of the "Actions to Take" section of the list–#33 "Grandpa Day".

GET CREATIVE

25. Video Messages
^Top Five Pick!^

Similar to writing letters to certain people in your life or for special, upcoming days (see #2 above) recording video messages can powerfully extend your presence and help you find meaning. With modern technology, these can easily be saved for viewing in the future. Just be sure to share the location and any needed password information with a person who can then share these videos for a long time to come.

26. Guided Journals

Perhaps you want to share some words, but you aren't much for writing or putting words together. Many good guided journals have page after page of prompts for you to record everything from some favorite memories to what kind of clothes you liked to wear when you were in high school. These tools can help you tell your story in an organized way when you aren't sure where to start.[5]

27. Story Telling

Reminiscence is always powerful. We will talk more about rumination at the beginning of the "Actions to Take" section of the list. Nostalgia can be a treasured gift. There are fundamental stories, some which are wrought with power, others funny and quirky, which should not die with you. I recently told my teenage son a story about his grandpa, my dad.

When I was a teen myself, I once mowed the grass at our suburban home.

Exactly once.

I thought I did an acceptable job. My dad disagreed. He didn't yell at, complain to, or demean me. He simply never asked me to mow the grass again.

However, my dad also oversaw the property of our Catholic Church. The property contained several acres that needed to be mowed often.

With a large riding lawnmower.

For years my dad paid me (quite well) for mowing those acres at church, even though I was deemed unfit to care for the family lawn.

I love this story, though I am not sure why. I think because it shows some things about my dad. He is particular, but he was not condemnatory. Additionally, he didn't mind paying me well to do an important job.

This story also says a little something about me. I had a pretty easy upbringing. And I liked to work, do a good job, and earn money. It's not a big story. It's not about migration to a new country, leaving the family farm, or getting a degree, but I like this story.

Chances are you have stories like this one about my mowing prowess (or lack thereof). They tell something about you and others in your life.

Type them up. Re-tell them out loud to someone. Speak them into a device that will turn your verbal story into a text document that can be saved.

They may carry a weight that is invisible right now.

28. Genealogy Work

You know who your grandparents are and what is interesting about them, but your grandchildren will not unless you write their story.

Charting a bit of your family's history is easier than ever before. Even if you are adopted, records are more open to you today than they have been in the past.

Don't fear–much of this information is free and easily accessed. Some libraries with a genealogy department offer family history services.[6] You don't have to compile an exhaustive history of your family. Having just a small amount of information and some great anecdotes about a couple of generations will help find meaning in the sense of the permanence we talked about in chapter two.

29. Voice Recording Books

> **Seeing connections between generations alleviates the fear that the end of a life also means the end of *life*.**

One year for Christmas, my wife's parents gave our (then young) children a storybook. But this storybook had an added feature. Mimaw and Papaw were able to record their voices reading the lines on each page. So, when you turned one page you heard Papaw's warm and edgy voice (imagine how a man talks after years of working as a coach, teacher, and referee), and when you turned the next you heard Mimaw's mother-goose/girl scout leader voice reading the words on the page.

Perhaps creating something like this would give you a sense of meaning and keep your voice alive (quite literally) after you are gone.

PRAYERS TO PRAY

30. Pray for your own forgiveness
^Top Five Pick!^

Years ago, I was at work when I got a page saying that there was a patient who wanted prayer before surgery. While this type of task is what most people picture chaplains doing, we do much more in my health system (see the Preface), so calls like these are often a welcome relief.

The patient was pretty young, and the surgery was not terribly dramatic compared to many others that were happening that same day. However, he was scared.

We prayed that his fear would be eased, that his team would have God's help during the surgery, and that he would recover well afterward. I concluded our prayer and stood to leave. But I could tell he didn't feel any better than he had before I was paged. He still seemed agitated and fearful.

"Is there something else?" I asked.

He mustered his courage and said, "I don't know that I am saved. I went to church as a kid, and I prayed to accept God into my heart, but I have done a lot of living since then."

After a few more questions, I better understood what he meant by "being saved", and we prayed again. We prayed for God's forgiveness, allowing him to turn from his sin and accept the grace of God. This time, after we said "amen", he was like a new man. He had laid down the burden he was carrying. And you could see it.

Maybe, you still feel restless.

Maybe, the words you need to express are not to your loved ones, yourself, or your doctor. Maybe, you need to talk to God. Maybe, you need to pray for forgiveness.

31. Pray for Your Legacy

Pray for those who will follow you in this world. Project your heart and beliefs into the future by praying for those who will live in the future. Jesus prayed for those who would come after him, and you can, too.

32. Pray a Summary Prayer

Many hospice workers lead people in a beautiful activity called a 'life review'. It is what it sounds like, and I recommend you consider it. However, we can also review our lives in prayer before God.

Pray your honest feelings about your childhood, education, job, relationships, family or lack-thereof, sickness, successes, and failures.

33. Pray a Prayer of Thanks

Thanksgiving isn't the only time you can make a list of gifts for which you are thankful.

If you need a start, check out my video listed in the endnote below.[7]

34. Pray a Prayer of Blessing on Your Loved Ones

Many times throughout history, people have laid hands on others and prayed over them. Consider calling together a close group of friends to lay hands on them and pray for them. This can be done as a group or individually.

Plan the prayer ahead of time, even if you aren't used to doing that.

Finally, be sure to record the prayer somehow. Type it up, video record it, or use a well-known prayer that could be found again easily. Then, when others recall this moment, they will feel the weight and a sense of permanence.

+++

Remember Bethany.

Bethany was nearing the end of her life. In the end, she had about seven weeks. The first few weeks of the time she had left, she wrote letter after letter. To her husband and children, to her parents, and you.

When she was gone, those letters took on huge significance, and they made it seem as though she lived on, even though she was gone.

When we take time to express words, it helps us find meaning through weight (our words can mean so much) and permanence (capturing this piece of ourselves helps our presence to continue even when we can't be there.)

When you are searching for meaning, there might be words that need to be expressed.

You have something to say.

Will you say it?

Take a minute to skim back through the list and pick just one. Make a plan. Make a call. Better yet, just go ahead and do the one thing on this list you selected.

Do it today! This book will be here when you are done.

Notes

1. For a book about Funerals, read Dr. Jon Swanson's Giving a Life Meaning: *How to Lead Funerals, Memorial Services, and Celebrations of Life*. Jon is a trusted friend, and this is a trusted resource.

2. www.kateskart.org

3. See Appendix B for an important story about planning not only your finances but your medical care through Advance Care

Planning

4. Again, Dr. Swanson's book can help.

5. For a story of a woman named Lori whose journal saved her life, read *No Matter How Small*, by me and my wife, Kristen/

6. My hometown library (in Fort Wayne, Indiana, USA) has a world-renown genealogy department: http://www.genealogycenter.org/

7. Search YouTube for Parkview Health, Patrick Riecke, "10 Things to be Thankful For".

Case Study #2: Robert's Actions to Take

Robert is a military veteran. During his twenty-year career he was never in combat, but, like most soldiers, he lived in many different places.

Stationed overseas four times, Robert enjoyed some of his duty stations. Others he tolerated, always making the best of the situation.

"I can't complain," he would say. Then he added with a grin and a wink "Wouldn't do me any good anyway."

Born in the southern United States, his family was simple during his growing up years.

His dad worked at a local manufacturing plant and his mother kept the house and kids in line, as well as picking up part-time work now and then.

They attended a little church with white, wood siding, and a tall steeple. Robert always felt safe when his family walked through the doors of the church. The ladies of the church made great food and gave great hugs. The pastor walked with a cane and always had candy in his office.

When Robert was seven, the preacher gave a sermon about giving your heart to Jesus. He described Jesus as embracing his children with open arms.

As he sat next to his dad, a large man with long arms and bony, yet gentle hands, Robert could picture the arms of God wrapping around him.

Robert felt a warmth in his chest. He could feel the embrace of God. At seven-years-old, as he sat in that pew, Robert whispered to God, "I trust you."

His dad looked down, gave a wide smile, and squeezed Robert to his chest. That very morning Robert was baptized by the candy-pastor at that little white church.

+++

June's family attended the same little church, and she and Robert always found each other across the sanctuary on Sunday morning.

Many years later, Robert and June were married in that church, and the candy-pastor performed the ceremony. Their wedding came early in Robert's military career, but the couple put off having children for several years.

When they were finally ready to start their family, they had three boys in four years. June and the boys were left at home for one more overseas stint for Robert, but they exchanged letters constantly.

By the time the boys were nearing adolescence, Robert retired from the military, and they settled down in the town where Robert and June had grown up. Robert found work without too much trouble, and the boys adjusted nicely to the local schools. The boys all took to soccer pretty quickly, and before long, family weekends were spent at one soccer game after another.

When the oldest, William, was a senior in high school, the youngest, James, was a freshman. Michael, in the middle, was a junior. For one year, they were all on the same school team.

Robert and June were never more at home than when they were on the sidelines of those soccer games. They loved cheering all their children on at once.

Shortly after the boys began moving out and living on their own, June started having heart problems. She'd been sick a lot as a child, and her illnesses took a toll on her body.

In those days, open-heart surgery was still somewhat new. When June had surgery, they had to travel to find a surgeon who could do the operation.

Sadly, despite their best efforts, June lost her pulse during the surgery, and the staff could not revive her. Robert never forgot the feeling he had when the surgeon came into the room, peeled off his green sterile gloves, and shook his head. He put his hand on Robert's shoulder and told him he was sorry.

Robert made the long drive home alone. He called his boys and their families together and gave them the news. It was the most difficult few days, weeks, and months of his life.

As the next few years went on, buoyed somewhat by the new introduction of grandchildren, Robert soldiered on.

+++

Now, Robert is old.

He knows that life is a gift. He also knows that his doctor recently gave him some news about his health that he hasn't yet shared with his sons. He knows that not only is life a gift—in his case, it's a limited-time offer.

That has Robert thinking.

He's been thinking about his childhood, his military career, about June, and the boys. About the different chapters of his life.

After a lot of thought, Robert calls his son Michael and makes the announcement. Not about the news from the doctor. But about his plans during this limited time. "I'm going on tour again, son."

"On tour, dad? What do you mean?"

"I'm going to see all the important places. You know, before I'm dead." He chuckles, then takes advantage of Michael's stunned silence. He speaks quickly in choppy sentences.

"Two spots overseas where I was stationed. I loved both of them. And I'm going back for a visit to each of them. I'm going to be a week in both places–one after the other. I bought my tickets just this morning."

He's on a roll and continues before Michael can figure out what questions to ask.

"After that, I am going to come back home and visit the rest of the important places. I want you to go with me to some of them. I'll tell your brothers, too. Just thought you should know."

+++

True to his word, Robert leaves a couple of months later for his two destinations in other countries. When he returns he has picture after picture to show his grandchildren. His sons seem a little bewildered and even concerned about their dad. But, he made it there and back, so they are thankful, and a little impressed.

After dinner, dessert, and more pictures, the smaller kids run off to play.

Robert sinks back in the big cushions of the blue-gray couch in William's living room.

The brothers all exchange a glance. They are all thinking the same thing. Dad looks tired. Not just because he took a long trip, but tired on a deeper level.

"What's next, pops?" asks his youngest son as he sips crimson wine.

"Basic training," Robert replies.

"I think you're a little too old for that, Gramps." A grandson chimes in as he passes through the family room.

Robert mimes a salute and gives a smile before the boy leaves the room.

"No, I mean I want to visit the base where I did my basic training years ago." Robert clarifies.

Michael pipes up, "I'm going that way to take Callie back to college in two weeks. We'll take you then."

And they do.

Robert tells Michael and Callie one story after another from his short time at the base. They encounter several officers and many enlisted men and women who patiently listen to Robert's memories. They spend the night and visit the grounds again early the next morning, before taking Callie back to school.

+++

After two trips overseas and one to his military base, the rest of Robert's "important places" are all nearby.

He goes by his childhood home. Later, he wished he had skipped that spot because the house was broken down and unoccupied. The whole street, where he played as a child, was an eyesore.

He stopped by schools and grocery stores, sometimes by himself, and sometimes with family.

He visited the spot where he and June had their first date. Callie was home on a school break and drove him to the ice cream shop, still in operation all these years later. Robert was glad Callie was home because she had always reminded him of June. She had her grandmother's spirit and smile. In fact, he called her "June 2.0".

It was while they were having ice cream that Robert's tears finally surfaced. Visiting a spot that held the memory of a beginning... and knowing that June's end came too terribly soon, was almost too much to bear. All poor Callie could do was hug grandpa and share a few of her tears with him. She'd never seen him so sad. Still, when she dropped him off back at home, he could not thank her enough for the special afternoon.

That weekend, he told his boys that he wanted them to go with him to the last two important places on his "before I die" list, as he had started calling it, always with a chuckle.

After having an early breakfast together on a mild Spring morning, the four men drove the short distance to the high school soccer field. William had a soccer ball in the back of his car. As they kicked the ball around, Robert made several comments about how they were "much better athletes in high school." There was a lot of laughing, and they lost count of how many times stories started with the phrase, "Remember the time...?"

Eventually, James turned to his dad and picked up the ball.

"Well, pops, you said there was one more place. Where are we headed next?"

"Follow me," he said.

They walked through the parking lot, angling away from the school. James knew immediately where they were going and it didn't take long for William and Michael to catch on. Even though dad hadn't been forthright about the news from the doctor, they were catching on to that part as well.

They crossed the street at a stoplight and turned left. Just ahead, a dilapidated white steeple rose against the horizon.

"Dad," James said, hesitantly. "You know the church is closed down, right?"

Robert didn't answer. He was walking ahead of them. His gaze was the most intense they had seen in a long time.

After a few blocks, there they were; in the gravel parking lot, dotted with green and yellow weeds, where Robert's family used to park when they went to church.

Not much was said at first, although Robert did share a few memories.

It was while William was looking through an old window, trying to catch a glimpse of the sanctuary, that they heard a voice from behind them.

"Can I help you, gentlemen?" As they turned, they saw a man a little older than William walking toward them.

"I'm sorry, sir. We aren't trying to cause any trouble. My dad attended this church when he was a boy." William had blushed a little because of how he was straining to see inside the church, pulling himself up on the exterior of the building.

"How do you do?" Robert held out his hand.

"My name's Gordon." The man replied.

Robert seemed to have been looking for an excuse to tell his story, and now Gordon's presence seemed like the perfect opportunity.

Robert told him about his dad, his mom, and June. He told him about his Sunday school classes and the hymns they used to sing in that church. He told him about church meals and the food he enjoyed.

Then he came to the story he really wanted to tell–the story about hearing the candy-pastor tell about an embracing God, and the warmth he had felt in his chest that had stayed with him throughout his entire life. When Robert told him he was baptized that day, he reached into his pocket and pulled out a small piece of paper that was yellowed with age.

It was his baptismal certificate.

The brothers exchanged looks again.

He pointed at the bottom where the pastor had signed.

William, James, and Michael were all listening closely, but they were surprised at how closely this fellow, Gordon, was listening as well.

When Robert pointed to the pastor's name he read it out loud.

"Reverend David L. Peabody."

Gordon held the paper in his hands.

After a short pause, he looked up at Robert and his sons.

"Sir, my full name is Gordon Peabody. Your pastor was my grandfather."

"No kidding!" Robert didn't seem quite as shocked as the boys were.

"No kidding." Gordon smiled widely. "We moved into the old parsonage about ten years ago when the church closed down. Been keeping an eye on the property ever since."

That's when it dawned on Gordon.

"I have the keys. Would you like to go inside?"

Robert's voice trembled ever so slightly. "Would I ever."

Moments later, Gordon returned with a tangle of keys and let them inside. After slowly moving through the foyer and classrooms, the five men entered the sanctuary. Although covered with a thick layer of dust, the church was still a beautiful place filled with wood fixtures, old books, and light streaming through the windows that lined each side of the sanctuary.

Robert walked over to a pew on the left and sat down. He felt like a boy again. He could feel his dad seated next to him. Leaning forward, he looked toward the back of the church, where a little girl named June always sat with her mom. Tears brimmed, and his boys tried not to display that they were watching their dad closely.

Robert turned back to the front of the sanctuary again and squeezed his eyes shut, which released a tear running down his right cheek like a silent streak of lightning.

In the very spot where he had prayed the same words when he was seven-years-old, Robert said to God again, "I trust you."

It was a quiet, sacred moment.

After some more stories, Gordon walked over to a stack of old hymnals and handed one to Robert.

"Here," he said. "Please keep this. I want you to have it."

+++

Five months later, on a beautiful Sunday morning in Autumn, Robert did not wake up. After trying to call several times, James finally went to his dad's house. His dad looked like he was sleeping in the bed.

As James waited for more family to arrive at the house, he sat down on his dad's bed. He held his dad's hand. He had suspected his dad knew this day was coming, and he was right.

That's when he noticed the old hymnal sitting on the nightstand. He opened it slowly and leafed through the songs. A few days later, at the funeral, he tucked the hymnal into the casket with Robert, next to the shoulder he used to look over to see pretty little June in the back of the church.

Michael said the last words before the casket was closed. "You did it pops. You visited all the important places before you died. Thanks for taking us along for the ride."

Actions To Take: 33 More Ways to Find Meaning

The word bequest means to leave a meaningful gift–and the category of gifts we discussed in the last chapter was the gift of *words to express*. Everything from telling a story to composing videos can be benedictions that give us a sense of continuation of our lives beyond our deaths.

Sometimes, to tap into meaning, to feel the weight of a situation, we need to do something more than just talk or pray. Like Robert, we need to *take action*. This part of the list will help you find ways to take those actions. A handful of these actions are recommended as "Maximum Impact Ideas". Unlike the "Top Five Picks" in the last section, these are not actions everyone can take. They are some of the most difficult items on the list. However, they will make a major impact. Below are thirty-three actions you can take to find meaning in your specific life.

RUMINATION STATION

1. Ruminate on Your Hardest Moments

Phase Two is all about overcoming hardships. Chances are, if I asked you to list off some of the hardships you've had in your life, you could quickly begin listing one after another.

The beautiful thing about Phase Two is that we *do* face hard times, but we *do* overcome. That can give us a sense of meaning as well. Meaning, of course, isn't *only* found in Phase Three. It's just that the theme of Phase Two is *help*, while the theme of Phase Three is *meaning*.

We often find meaning when we can look back on hard times and realize that God was good, or that we made it through, or that others helped us.

While I don't encourage you to think too deeply about the most painful aspects of your life without some good assistance from a counselor or other professional, ruminating on how you have made it through hard times can be done simply, and you can draw a lot of strength. When we ruminate we purposefully think over the events. We remember how we felt. We consider how those events and feelings affected us from that point on. Start by ruminating on the hardships you have overcome.

2. Ruminate on Trouble

While getting caught skipping school isn't funny when you are a teenager, if you are in your 80s and thinking back on it, your childhood mischief can create excitement and amusement.

3. Allow Others to Serve You

Allow others to serve you in your need. Drop your pride, and realize that there might be people who *want* to help you. Serving you allows them to find meaning in your suffering–suffering they are likely sharing with you.

4. Ruminate on the Funniest Moments

Think of when you laughed, really laughed, whether around a dinner table, in a classroom, at a movie theater. Ruminating means turning the scene over and over in your mind. When you add gratitude to the rumination, it can amplify the initial effect of that enjoyable situation.

5. Remember Jesus
Maximum Impact Idea

If you are a believer in Jesus, or even if you aren't, read the story of the death of Jesus and for an extended rumination on the sufferings of Jesus, what he teaches us about both Phase Three and finding meaning in suffering, visit the postscript of this book.

For now, if you need a companion along life's journey (all the way to death), Jesus is ready and waiting in the pages of the Christian sacred book.

6. Practice Mindfulness

Practice mindfulness while you are sick. Try to be fully present instead of wanting to run away (like we usually do).

A friend explained to me that mindfulness is a hard thing to *start* when you are sick, but if you have any experience with this technique before this situation, lean into it again.

7. Embrace Visions and Dreams
Maximum Impact Idea

Often there is something mystical and mysterious that occurs as our life ebbs away. I like to say that the veil thins between our physical world and the spiritual world.

This can lead to vivid dreams. Many people have reported seeing and experiencing things that are unexplainable as they face their mortality.

If you have dreams and visions (visions are like dreams when you are awake) while you are in Phase Three, don't run from the experience.

8. Religious Rites

Clergy from many of the world religions have visited our hospital to perform religious rites for our patients. These can be extremely meaningful. They carry weight. You sense they are connected to something with eternal significance. They also have permanence, because many of them have been in place for hundreds or thousands of years.

9. Go and Apologize

If a person comes to mind when you read the phrase "go and apologize", then you know what you need to do.

GIVE IT AWAY

10. Give Stuff Away

You may have a wonderful mental picture to think about your loved ones having some of your possessions after you are gone, but is that antique clock really bringing you that much joy right now? If it is, then great, keep it right where it is.

If not, then maybe it's time *now* to give it to your great-niece. Then you can tell her how to wind it, who has fixed it for you in the past, and where you got it.

11. Your Car
Maximum Impact Idea

I had two very different, but related, experiences within a short time.

First, a good friend and colleague of mine died from the flu. While that is a really short sentence, you can imagine the sorrow and pain that her death caused. She was one of the best people I have ever known.

While she was in the hospital, her sister was running through the questions that come up when a young person dies. One of her questions was "what are we going to do with her car?"

Second, I was a keynote speaker at a conference for a couple of hundred professionals. The conference was held at a local retirement home. As I was walking in with my computer, books, and materials in hand, I passed by the parking places for residents. There I saw a Chevrolet Corvette from the 1970s. It was red, with a black convertible top and flip-up headlights. It was in perfect condition, except it was covered in a thick layer of dust. It was an opportunity being missed right there in the parking lot.

Your car might not be a pristine Corvette (neither is mine). But it might have value to someone, more than you realize.

If there isn't someone in your life that would use it, there are always organizations that will gladly accept your car or boat as a donation.

This will, again, give you a sense of increased permanence, your life continuing past the confines of your years on earth.

12. Consider Your Collections

My mother-in-law has a collection of Christmas village pieces (little ceramic houses, fences, people, a church, etc.) My dad has a collection of festival buttons. Touching the buttons, setting up the village, gives a sense of connectedness to each of them.

Passing them along to others, or at least making plans to do so, gives them a sense of connectedness to us and the future.

13. Holiday Decorations

For many cultures, those items that we put out at certain times of the year carry a huge emotional weight. Their meaning is attached to their permanence. The star on top of the Christmas tree just keeps showing up. The family menorah climbs up on to the mantel every year. The football-themed kitchen towels slip out of hiding as the sport fires up each autumn.

Is there someone who would resonate deeply with a gift of decorations? Make the transition now, or plan for it. Your life (and love) will remain with them through those mementos for years.

14. Remember the Ring
Maximum Impact Idea

Many people in the world today are wearing grandma's ring. Or grandpa's medal. While these items might have monetary value, their meaning value can be even higher.

My father-in-law wears a St. Christopher medal everywhere he goes. It's not just a necklace. It represents him. I am guessing it will end up around the neck of one of his loved ones years from now.[1] And in that way, he will remain with them; he will gain permanence.

Maybe you don't wear anything special. But you could start. If you are in Phase Three and the end of your own life is coming, is there an article of clothing or an accessory that you could wear regularly, have your picture taken with, and then give to someone so that you maintain permanence after you are gone from this world?

15. The Shirt off Your Back

It may seem silly or even a little too personal, but when you die (whether that's in the near or the distant future), what will become of your wardrobe?

Don't let it just get tossed away. Share some things purposefully.

If you don't have a loved one you want to share your clothes with, pick a favorite charity or have them transformed into a stuffed animal, pillow, or quilt.

ROAD TRIP!

16. Visit Your Childhood Home

Was there a house you lived in when you were younger that holds some meaning for you? What if you drove by? Or even knocked on the door?

If you can't drive by because of distance or other reasons, do you have some pictures of the home that you could ruminate on? Maybe you can search for the location online and find some quality images. Gazing at the image of a place where you lived in the past can connect you to that past.

And connecting with the past feels very similar to connecting to the future.

Remember the theme verse for Phase Three. "God has set eternity in the heart of man, and yet we cannot fathom what God has done from beginning to end."

Not being able to fathom something doesn't mean we can't appreciate it and ruminate on it.

17. Revisit Religiously Significant Locations

Were you baptized in a certain place? Did you come to faith in a certain city?

The moment that God became real to me wasn't at the Catholic church where I grew up or the Evangelical church I transitioned to later.

It was on a park bench when an old man stopped to talk with me about Jesus. I've revisited this site many times, even though I am not imminently dying (that I know of); and when I do, I feel a connection with the eternity that God has set in the human heart.

18. Revisit Your Wedding Site

Stand in the place where your sweetheart became your spouse.

19. Revisit the Place you Became a Parent

This is easier when you work at the hospital where two of your four children were born (like I do).

About twice a week I see a family walking out of our Family Birthing Center with a little one in a seat, balloons, and bags, and I am taken back to the moments when two of our boys went home for the first time.

Would it feel like it had weight or meaning to revisit the place where your child or children were born? What about the place where you were born?

20. Visit Other Past Homes or Schools

Not just your childhood home or homes. Every previous home symbolizes a part of your life. Was there a school that was meaningful to you? Visit and take some pictures. Better yet, call ahead and see if you can go in, visit the classroom where you fell in love, learned something significant, or discovered art.

Being connected to the past makes us feel connected to the greater arc of history, which gives us a sense of permanence that we may need when we face the meaningless feelings that can accompany Phase Three.

21. Visit the Place Where You Became You
Maximum Impact Idea

We had just had our fourth child when I graduated from Seminary. I was wandering a bit in my ministry, not sure what to do next.

As I sat with the other graduates during commencement, I received an award for how I led my church. I had been told ahead of time that I was getting that award. However, as I sat back down, they began describing the next award and recipient. I was so busy looking at my first award that I didn't realize they were talking about me again until the professor said, "And this award *also* goes to Patrick Riecke."

I was dumbfounded. I'd never really won anything before.

And I hadn't *won* these. I had *earned* them.

At that moment, I stopped viewing myself as less significant than everyone else around me and started thinking of myself as good enough after all.

I've never gone back to that building.

But I guarantee when I do, I will feel the weight.

Is there a place where you became who you are today?

A spot on the playground where you stood up for yourself? The spot where you gave your first talk or fixed your first car?

Consider revisiting that site.

22. Take a Ride in (or Buy!) Your Favorite Car

As a father of four children, I've owned aggravatingly sensible cars for a very long time.

However, for my third son's tenth birthday, we visited a specialty car lot. This car lot has classic cars, race cars, and many price tags that have more zeroes than my annual salary. We both gaped at vehicle after vehicle. He especially loves antique trucks, and I love old sports cars.

It was a slow day at the car lot, and one of the salesmen learned that it was Levi's birthday.

"Wanna go for a ride in the Hellcat?" he asked Levi.

Levi had probably never heard the word "Hellcat" until that moment; but his eyes shot open, and he looked straight at me, full of excitement. I admit that I didn't know a Hellcat was a Dodge Challenger.

"It's the bright yellow one, right there…" He pointed through the window to a car that had high-back molded seats with harnesses instead of normal seat belts.

As Levi slid into the front seat of this totally-not-mom-approved vehicle, I realized there was no back seat. In other words, I would be sitting out for this ride.

As I watched my ten-year-old birthday boy fly out of the parking lot with a salesman whose name I couldn't remember ("Did he say his name was Rick? Scott?"), I started to question my decision-making as a father.

However, when he came back safe and sound (and with a smile that would not wipe away for the next few hours), I realized *riding* in the Hellcat made life shoot through him in a way that just *looking* at it didn't.

I realize that compared to some other items on this list like "making peace", car rides might seem superficial, but connecting to life in *any* way can bring a sense of weight and meaning.

23. Value Vacations

When a loved one dies, many people not only experience their home differently but also their vacation spots. If you often visited a certain location with family or friends, how should they think about that location if/when they visit again?

Could they take a picture in a certain spot and honor you, even if you can't be there?

Should they sell the vacation home and do something different with the money? Or keep it and enjoy it?

If you were the one that always loved going there and no one else did, can you permit them to avoid that spot in the future?

DECISIONS, DECISIONS

24. Decide Where to Die
Maximum Impact Idea

So many times this is a severely painful decision made in the worst possible moment. There are three main choices, and each has advantages and disadvantages.

1. **Home.** You can do this with the support of health professionals like in-home hospice or other healthcare. The advantage can be that it's more comfortable for the person who is dying and sometimes for the family, as well. Family can eat at home, sleep at home, and still be there for you. The disadvantage can be that your family or support people feel more responsibility to care for you since there isn't a constant professional presence. They might be happy to do that, or they might feel inadequate and anxious.

2. **Hospital.** At the hospital, you will have the highest level of professional support. However, not everyone is appropriate to stay at the hospital. In the modern healthcare world, you have to have a *reason* to be at the hospital, and just the fact that you are dying isn't always a qualifying reason. Some hospitals have hospice beds, and that can be an easier place (and more appropriate) to stay for a longer

99

time as death approaches. Another disadvantage is the obvious fact that it isn't home. Your family may have to travel back and forth, eat in the cafeteria or at restaurants, etc. Of course, the medical bill for a lengthy hospital stay can be expensive. Some hospitals are wonderfully supportive of their dying patients, while others aren't exactly sure what to do with them. Judge this by how the hospital makes you *feel,* not by their clinical qualifications alone.

3. **Other Healthcare Facility**. Hospice homes and skilled nursing facilities can be very supportive long-term environments. They have the constant healthcare presence like a hospital, but a more accessible environment intended to feel like home. Hospice homes are usually wonderfully supportive and, to be honest, people come there (usually) to die. So, they are well-equipped for this final journey. Some nursing homes are similarly supportive. However, remember to do your Advance Care Planning.[2] If your heart fails at the nursing home, do you want them to do CPR on you and rush you to the hospital? If so, make that clear. If not, make that clear.

This is a broad topic, so for more information, sign up today for my online course at PatrickRiecke.com/courses. Ultimately, of course, we don't always get to decide everything about our death, but one implication of the advances in healthcare is that we are living longer *with* sickness than ever before. That means that the end is less often abrupt and gives us chances to make choices about where we will die.

I've watched many family members debate, at the hospital bedside of their loved one, where they should move them in the last days of their life. That's not a good moment to have this debate, whether internally or as a group.[3]

25. Die on the Road

I don't recommend this. However, I am aware of one time it happened, and the story is quite inspiring.

Late one night we got a call that there was a dead person at one of our hospitals. More accurately, a person was dead in the *parking lot* of the hospital. In a car, a car that the family had been driving across the country. They were on a bucket-list trip for their grandmother. She was dying, but she had stuff she wanted to do (I think she would have liked Robert).

So, they set about doing those things.

Our hospital system is in the mid-west of the United States. They were coming back from someplace on the East coast and heading home.

Grandma had fallen asleep as people do in the car on a long trip.

But when they tried to wake her when they stopped near our hospital, the could not rouse her.

She had died on the road.

Again, while I don't recommend dying in a car under any circumstance, this elderly road warrior provides inspiration to take actions that help find meaning.

26. Fido and Fluffy

Worrying about what will happen to your pet(s) without you can be one of the worst parts of Phase Three. I can't tell you how many times we have facilitated a visit with a pet to see a dying patient in our hospital, and it's always meaningful.

If you have a pet, and you sense you might be in Phase Three, maybe you should start thinking about what is in the best interest of your pet.

GET CREATIVE

27. Get Musical

I'm not musical. Are you? If so, maybe it's time to write a song for someone special or write the lyrics of a song.

Twin babies died at our hospital. The only thing worse that one baby dying is two babies dying.

Our overnight chaplain was there for the family. He's musical. One morning I had a music file in my inbox from Michael, the chaplain. He had dedicated an instrumental song to the twins. He wrote it, performed it, and recorded it.

Since I am not a musician, I can't explain it, but the song truly reflects the pain of two babies dying in one family at the same time.

If you aren't a songwriter, maybe you just need to decide that there is a certain song that belongs to you and a special someone, so that whenever it comes on, you will live again.

28. Photo Shoot

I have a confession. I hate photoshoots. When our children were small, we would go to a local department store and sit in impossibly uncomfortable poses for what felt like hours to get the "perfect" photo. Of course, now, looking back at those pictures warms my heart.

I've had many people show me photos and say, "That's the last picture we took with mom."

Rather than a blurry, half-hearted final picture, plan a time to prepare, pick a spot, and make a memory.

29. Create a List of Absolute Truths about Life

What do you know for sure about the world, about life? In a 2017 TED Talk, author Anne Lamott shared her list of twelve truths.

Her list varies from the inane and silly (one is about the nature of chocolate) to the fundamental. Her twelfth truth is "Death happens and you'll never get over the loss of your loved ones, but they will live again in your heart if you don't seal it off (don't be scared of death, it's as sacred as birth)."[4]

If you had to create a list of things you know for sure about life, what would it include?

30. Create a List of Absolute Truths about God

My idea of God has shifted considerably as I have gone through many Phase Two experiences. Difficult times lead us to new truths, not just about life, but also about God, ourselves, and the nature of truth and reality.

Create a list of truths you know for sure about God (hint: shorter is probably better).

31. Create a List of Absolute Truths about Those Closest to You
Maximum Impact Idea

This idea is very specific. Remember, Frankl taught us that all meaning is concrete and specific to the individual.

Think of those closest to you. What do you know for sure about your mom? Co-worker or child? Spouse?

What would it look like to create a list of "Absolute Truths" about that person?

Here are a few of mine about my wife, Kristen:

1. Kristen Riecke *will* have high expectations and will probably be disappointed when things don't turn out quite right.

2. Kristen Riecke *will* remember you and *will* pray for you. Around a campfire in our backyard one evening she asked a friend how his grandfather was doing after his recent illness. Colton responded, "You must be thinking of someone else, my grandfather is fine." Kristen, inextricably, probed further. She was sure it was Colton's grandfather, even if Colton was sure it wasn't. Eventually, he said, "Oh, you know what, he did have a trip to the hospital several months ago for a heart issue, and I asked for prayer. I totally forgot about that." Kristen

105

will remember your need and pray for your need,
even if you don't remember that the need exists.

3. Kristen Riecke *will* cry with you. She has said that
   she probably could qualify as a professional mourner
   if anyone would hire her. She will probably cry
   when she reads these three bullet points.

32. Scents

The sense most strongly tied to memory is smell.

Do you wear the same perfume or cologne regularly?

Would it be meaningful to give someone intimately close to
you a bottle of your scent?

33. Grandpa Day
Maximum Impact Idea

A friend of mine lost her dad when her children (his
grandsons) were still very young. They felt the loss of his
presence deeply.

As they approached the first anniversary of grandpa's death,
her oldest son, Julian, had an idea. He suggested that they
gather the family on "Grandpa Day" and do things he liked to
do.

He liked to go to garage sales, visit G.I. Joe's Army Surplus Store, go to the zoo and eat coney dogs at a classic local hot dog stand. It's not surprising that they recalled stories about Grandpa all day.

What was surprising to them was that they could very much feel his presence with them all day.

Could you, now, start your loved ones thinking this way, so they have something more to look forward to?

+++

Remember Robert? He decided there were places he needed to visit. Duty stations, past schools, and homes, but mostly the school where his sons played soccer and the church where he met God and June, the love of his life.

Sometimes, to tap into meaning, to feel the weight of a situation, we need to do something more than just talk or pray. We need to *take action.*

Look back through this section of the list and select one action you can take. Decide how you will do it. Decide when you will do it.

It's never too early to take actions that will add meaning to your life or the lives of those around you. Whether you, like Robert, need to make a list of important places to revisit before you die, or you need to pick something else from this list, do it today.

Incidentally, I love talking with groups about finding meaning. If you'd like me to speak to *your* group, go to PatrickRiecke.com.

Notes

1. Or it will be buried with him. One way or another, it will have a sense of permanence.
2. See the Appendix on ACP in the back of this book.
3. This is one specific part of planning your future medical care. For a more full approach to the increasingly important topic of Advance Care Planning and a story to illustrate the significance, turn now to Appendix B.
4. https://www.ted.com/talks. Search "Anne Lamott.".

Case Study #3: George's Gifts to Provide

Mary had been a widow for six days when Andre first appeared in her front yard.

Not many people can imagine what Mary felt that first night at home by herself. Sure, she had spent nights there by herself when George was in the hospital, but this was different. George was gone now. Everything about that first night felt so…final. After decades of having George at her side, she felt so alone.

In the coming days, her thoughts were a blur. In the midst of the blur, several scenes flashed repeatedly. She could see George's face, young and fresh on their wedding day, looking into her eyes. She could see him at the dinner table with friends, laughing and joking. And she could see his face when he was sick and in pain.

Mary and George never had children. Many of their siblings had already died. Their parents had been gone for years.

As George became sicker, attending their social activities became more difficult. Now, it would be very difficult for Mary to muster the strength to re-engage in those activities without him.

Mary had retired from her career as a professor of history at the local college nearly fifteen years earlier, and she and George had enjoyed many adventures together since then.

When they were younger, Mary used to joke that if she died first, George would starve to death shortly thereafter. He did not cook, and he did not like to eat at restaurants. He was from a very frugal family, which was also why he did the couple's taxes and finances from the beginning.

Mary is sophisticated. She likes the theater, fashion, museums, and long books with no pictures.

George was more practical and particular. He liked numbers and finishing little jobs at home and work. So, it was only natural that George was always the one who took care of the lawn and the car as well.

Now that George was gone, these were the three things that keep coming up in Mary's mind.

The yard.

The car.

The taxes.

The day after George's funeral was nearly enough to crush Mary. She had seen some old friends at the viewing and the funeral, but now, she felt, everyone else was returning to their "normal" lives. However, she knew, deep inside, that she never would.

It was a Saturday in the summer. In the past, this would have been a great time for her and George to have an adventure. Maybe a road trip or just a walk through their neighborhood.

But not today. Mary's thoughts were spinning again. Her mind was jumping from the emptiness she felt to the quietness in the house. Then from the finances to the yard, to the car and back again. She could feel herself losing her grip on her emotions. Suddenly, her thoughts were interrupted by a roar from outside her front window.

She stood and walked across the room and peered outside.

In her yard stood Andre, a boy about eleven-years-old from down the street.

She and George had always admired Andre. He came to their house when he was selling items to raise money for school or sports. Normally George hated it when solicitors came to the door, but he had a soft spot for kids raising money for activities. Plus Andre had an effusive personality.

One day, Mary came home from the store to find three large tins of popcorn on the kitchen island.

"George?" She called. "Where did all this popcorn come from?"

George came in from the study. Taking off his glasses, he asked, "You remember Andre from down the street? He came by and was carrying all three of these!" He shook his head and smiled. "We chatted about his football team, school, and his family. Somehow, when he left, he had my money and I had his popcorn."

George turned and started walking to the garage to help Mary carry in bags from the grocery.

"But you don't even like popcorn!" She called after him as he walked away.

+++

Now Andre stood in her front yard.

On the driveway behind him sat a small red gas can and a roar came from the lawnmower he was pushing across Mary's front yard. The grass was a little long. He was going slow and being careful.

Mary was puzzled but went to the kitchen and made a tall pitcher of cold lemonade. Then, she found her purse in the hall and pulled out some cash to give Andre when he was through.

About an hour later, when the sound from the mower came to a stop, Mary hopped up. She grabbed a tall glass of lemonade and the money and headed out the front door.

Andre accepted the lemonade and smiled at Mary. After she had thanked him several times, she held out the money she had gotten from her purse.

"Ma'am?" Andre said. "Your husband already paid me."

Mary's eyes widened.

"Honey, that's not possible. He died just last week."

"I know, ma'am. My father told me. That's why I am here."

"Your father told you to come to mow my lawn? That's very sweet, but I *do* want to pay you." Mary said.

"But, it's like I told you, your husband already paid me." He replied.

Now Mary looked completely confused and set her hands in her lap.

Andre could tell she wanted an explanation. He set down his glass and launched into a story he had figured she already knew.

"A couple of months ago, our doorbell rang. My dad answered. It was your husband. He didn't look like he felt very well, but he leaned around my dad and winked at me while I was doing my schoolwork." Andre took a sip of lemonade.

"After he left, my dad asked me to sit down. That's when he told me that your husband was sick. I still didn't know why he rang our doorbell, but my dad pulled a piece of paper out of his pocket. It was a check with your husband's name on it, for my dad. Then he explained to me that your husband wanted to hire me to mow your grass after he..." Andre paused.

"After he died?" asked Mary, wanting Andre to continue the story.

"Yes ma'am." Andre looked down, realizing he had been talking too fast. He took another sip of the lemonade and brought his story to a close. "He paid me to do this for the next two summers." He said slowly, looking at Mary's face. But when a new thought entered his mind, he started speaking quickly again. "But I'll do it till I'm an old man, just like your husband." He looked back at the well-mowed lawn. Then turned back to Mary. "It makes me proud. Makes me…"

"Happy," said Mary.

"Yes ma'am," said Andre.

After they said their goodbyes, Mary went back inside the house. As she entered the study, her eyes landed on a picture in which George had a wide smile—like he was laughing. She pretended she was mad at him. "Oh, you think you pulled one over on me, don't you? Thought you knew just what I might need when you were gone, did you? Well… sweetie… you weren't wrong. Thank you. I love you."

Andre was as good as his word, and quite a good little lawnmower—quite *particular.* Mary always liked seeing the grass get longer because it meant that Andre would be by soon, often along with a couple of his family members.

+++

George had two more surprises in store for Mary. Two more opportunities for her to 'yell' at the picture of him laughing.

About two months after George died, Mary's phone rang with a number she recognized. It was the business number of a local auto service shop. It was a very small shop, and for many years George trusted the man who ran it.

"Mary, I don't think we have met since George was always the one bringing the car in, but my name's Denny."

Denny cleared his throat and continued.

"A while back George stopped in with a proposal." Mary had just set out the pitcher to start making lemonade for the next time Andre would come by. Her eyes unconsciously shot over to the lemonade pitcher when Denny told a story about George setting up regular maintenance on the car and prepaying the whole thing for a long time to come.

George had taken care of the yard with the help of Andre.

George had taken care of the car with the help of Denny.

Mary's final surprise from George came in mid-January, about the time Mary started worrying about tax season. It had been a while since Mary had seen Andre and his family, although she had agreed to watch their dog for them when they went on an upcoming adventure. This time when her phone rang and a local trusted tax-preparer started telling her about a visit from George, Mary walked right into the study, looked at the "laughing George" picture, and started wagging her finger. "You did it, you got me again!" She said out loud, while the woman with the tax agency was still on the phone.

"I'm sorry ma'am?" She sounded confused.

"Oh, nothing. It's just that George still seems to be very much present with me in times like this. It helps. Otherwise, I would feel so alone." Mary tried to explain about Andre and Denny, but felt like it probably sounded like a jumbled mess of words. When she finished, the woman paused before replying.

"I understand, a least a little... My mom died two years ago, and I still feel her absence every day... Say, when we get together for me to help you with your taxes, how about we grab lunch instead of just meeting here in my office?"

Mary was surprised by the suggestion but graciously agreed.

That lunch appointment was the first of many. They talked about taxes for about ten minutes. Then they talked about George, the woman's mother, and their journeys since their deaths, and lost all track of time.

When she returned after that first lunch, she did not yell at George's picture. She held it and laughed. Then cried. Then laughed some more.

Gifts to Provide: 34 More Ways to Find Meaning

So far, we have discovered ways to find meaning through words to express and actions to take. Now, we turn our attention to *gifts* we can *provide,* the truest form of a bequest.

For most items on this list, there is a monetary requirement. (Meaning you will have to find a way to pay for the gift.) Don't let that scare you. Some of the items are free or very inexpensive–less than paying for a family meal at a restaurant. Others are higher cost, but also worth considering for their meaning.

Remember, as we reach the end of our lives, finances can turn upside down. Often that makes spending money more difficult, but at other times it can open up sources of finances that would not have made sense before. If you have a home, vehicle, or another item that means less to you now as you face a chronic or terminal illness or old age, perhaps you can liquidate it to provide for an item on this list that would help you experience a sense of weight or permanence. Maybe you can look ahead to life insurance and make plans for purchases. Maybe you can make a different choice for your healthcare to save money—a change from a hospital to a facility with a lower cost or to home can save a significant amount of money.

Lastly, before we consider this list, you may feel as though you are truly without funds or resources in any way. Let me encourage you. God owns everything, and he cares for you. The book of Psalms says that the cattle on a thousand hills belong to God.[1] God also says that the death of people is precious in his eyes—not that God causes people to die, but that he cares deeply for us as we face death and grief.[2] Perhaps, you do not have resources, but perhaps, there are resources available. Whether it's a not-for-profit, friends, a healthcare institution, a place of worship, or a crowd of people wanting to help someone fulfill their wish to give a gift to someone special, God may provide for you. So, even if you feel penniless, please don't skip this special section. A scale will be provided to help identify high-cost ideas and low-cost (or free) ideas.[3]

LEAVE A LEGACY

1. Write it in Stone

After my nephew's daughter was stillborn, our family went together to donate to our local children's zoo.[4] The donation qualified to have a brick inscribed. My sister selected a beautiful message. Now, every time our family visits the zoo, we also visit a tangible remembrance of Baby Delaney. Knowing that Delaney's brother and sister often visit the zoo and place their hands on this brick, we all feel connected. Connected not only to her little life but to one another as well. Plus, on another level, we feel she is connected to each visitor to the zoo.

These sorts of gifts can be selected at any time, not only after someone has died. Is there a non-profit that you could donate to and have something of weight and significance inscribed so that it can be a touch-point of connection for many years to come?

$ $

2. Donate to a Cause you Believe In

Do you think medical research is really important? Wigs for breast cancer patients? Providing homes for cats? Individuals aren't the only option when it comes to providing gifts that help us find meaning.

From a small donation to a substantial gift, this can help you feel as though your reach continues well past the edges of your life on earth.

$ – $ $ $ $

3. Underwrite Programming

Many non-profit organizations have programming that you can underwrite. The beauty of underwriting programming instead of just donating is that your name will be spoken out loud after you are gone.

How significant might it feel to have your loved ones hear your name and your dedication to a cause after you are gone? Whether it's over the radio waves or at the next charity event, this is a great way to provide some permanence.

$ $

4. Trust the Process

Each year in our community, there is a trust that gives generous awards to four recipients. The recipients are selected from four local not-for-profit organizations, one of which is the healthcare system I serve. I have the opportunity to sift through nominations and help select our recipient.

The story goes that many years ago the man for whom the trust is named was facing the end of his life. He was a single man with no children. His parents had left him a large fortune, and he had added to it over his lifetime.

When he died, he left the bulk of his estate to a trust to be managed and awarded annually to people who benefit our community in a tangible, service-oriented way; people who exemplify the values of one of these four organizations.

It's a beautiful experience year after year, mostly because the recipients are never people who expect to be recognized and are flabbergasted that they are selected.

It's unlikely that your parents left you a large fortune and you are pining to find a recipient. However, trusts can be set up for many purposes and with a wide variety of amounts.

$ $ $ – $ $ $ $

5. Save for College

If there is a young person in your life, consider setting up a college savings account. In many places, these are some of the easiest accounts to set up. Accounts can be established with very small amounts, have very little restrictions on the future use by the child, and also offer great tax advantages.

A general rule is to invest early for a young person. If you invest today for an infant, current projections are that your money will more than triple by the time they go to university.

Not only will this be a blessing to that child, but every single time they check the balance, they will remember your generosity.

$ $ – $ $ $ $

6. Take a Trip

In the section on *words to express,* we considered talking with our loved ones about what they can/should do about vacation spots in the future.

What if you could purchase a vacation package for them to enjoy? Could you send them to an amusement park or on a camping trip, on your dime?

A wonderful colleague of mine (who is not dying) has told his family he wants his ashes spread at a certain vacation location. That way, they will have to follow through on taking an important trip if they want to fulfill his wishes.

In whatever way you encourage, chances are you will live on in their conversations while they are on that trip, and talk about you with their friends and family as they prepare and even after they return.

$ $ $ $

7. Make Baby Blankets in Advance

Kristen has a handmade afghan that her paternal grandmother made for her. Each of Kristen's six siblings has one, too, as well as her one million cousins.

As of this writing, her grandmother is still alive, well into her 90s. She has continued making blankets. Each of our children has one, and she has a collection in reserve for future, unknown babies.

The family has plans that, at her funeral, they will take a photo of everyone with their blankets from grandma.

They'll need a wide-angle lens.

What do you make? Maybe it's not blankets, but is there something you could make to pass around now, and later?

$

8. Dear Diary

Have you written in a diary in the past? Who could be trusted with that sacred text? You might think it's not worth much, but it could mean the world to someone who will feel a loss when you are gone.

Oh, but don't just hand it over if you can help it. Wrap up your diaries, put a bow on them, write an intro note, and make a presentation out of it.

FREE

9. Pricey Possession

The value of a diary cannot be put into dollars and cents, but maybe you have something else that can be valued in dollars quite easily; an expensive painting, vehicle, appliance, or piece of technology.

If you are still very much enjoying that item—then please—enjoy it. But maybe give someone else who would enjoy it a 'gift card' telling them that if anything ever happens to you, it's her's. (Be sure to indicate this to the person who will execute your will.) You don't want them to look forward to your death just so they can have your pricey possession, but it can add some sweetness to their bitter loss.

FREE

SWEET AND SENTIMENTAL

10. Flowers Forever

Flowers mean life. They make most people smile. Perhaps you have a habit of getting flowers for someone special in your life at certain times or on special days.

Pick a florist in your area who has a long history and a seemingly stable future. Ask them if you could talk with them about a special, long-range project. Perhaps you want your spouse to get flowers every year on your anniversary for as long as they live. Or maybe you want your daughter to get flowers on Mother's Day.

First warning, you will probably make the florist cry. Florists are known to be caring and sensitive, so you might have to brace yourself for their response.

Secondly, chances are they have never done anything like this, so give them some grace to figure it out. Prepare for the arrangements and give them ideas of what you want based on what is usually in season at that time.

Imagine that special someone being surprised year after year, and having the sense that your presence continues.

$ $ $ $

11. Christmas Future

A couple of times I've heard of families celebrating a holiday after a loved one has died and experiencing a very concrete sense of the deceased loved one's presence at the celebration. The experience has taken the form of pre-purchased gifts for children and others. Families around a Christmas tree have opened gifts from a father who died just a few days before.

Providing this gift–the gift itself, the pictures, the memories, and the opportunity for conversation–could be one of the most weighty ideas on the list.

$ – $ $ $

12. Plant a Tree

Many of us had a tree in our lives as children that grew along with us. Whether it was at grandma's house, at a park, or in our backyard, the growth of the tree was observable and significant.

What if you bought a tree for a person or family and had it planted in a special place? People could visit that tree, take pictures, and have a special place to feel your presence, even after you're gone.

$ $ $

13. Be a Star

Maybe you can't be a star, but at least name one after yourself or someone else. If someone in your life is celestially-minded, they might love knowing that you are a part of an official star name registry.

$ – $ $

14. Re-purpose that Picture

Do you have a photo of yourself with someone(s) special? Maybe it's in print already, or maybe it's digital. Get your hands on it, and do something special with it. Blow it up huge, put it in a special frame, or make a pillow out of it.

FREE – $

15. Free Hugs

If you are sick, injured, or even just old, people can shy away from touching you. Who cares, though? Go hug them; a real hug. Embrace until they are totally uncomfortable or just super thankful.

While we are talking hugs, let's just talk love. Purposefully, I'm not spending a lot of time talking about love directly. That's because I figure you probably aren't struggling with loving people if you are doing any of this work I am recommending.

However, before you hug everyone who runs across your path, maybe it's good to take a few moments to think of the love you have in your heart for a few people who are close to you.

It's easy.

Think of the person or people.

Picture them in your mind.

Now color that picture with love.

And keep looking at them…
FREE

JUST FOR FUN

16. The Gift of Fun

One family whose child stayed in our pediatric unit after a scary motor vehicle crash felt that they received excellent care. Thankfully, the children and adults all eventually recovered from their injuries. However, their hearts were permanently touched by the care they had been given.

In a desire to pay the experience forward, they donated a full-sized arcade game to our pediatric unit.

After an interview with the mother, she said, "We hope the arcade gaming unit will provide a happy distraction for those [children] as well as their visiting family members. We certainly hope that it blesses everyone who plays it!"[5]

How could you give the gift of fun? Maybe you could purchase a large yard game, board game, or a jet ski?

Imagine people enjoying that for years to come–you are a part of that!
$ – $ $ $ $

17. The Gift of Your Favorite Restaurant

Do you have a favorite place to eat? Maybe some memories are special to you and your loved ones that were made at that restaurant. Did you celebrate someone's new job at a local eatery, or visit a certain restaurant every time a family member came to visit?

Purchase a handful of gift cards for that location. When they dine there (on you!) they will feel connected to you, and you will, in a very real way, still be present with them.

$ $

18. Kitchen-ware

Giving your sweetie a blender for your anniversary is not a good idea, but if you and your daughter both love coffee and you've always wanted a real espresso machine, go ahead and get it for her now. Then, every time she uses it, she will feel a connection to you whether you are in heaven or the kitchen with her. Not a coffee fan? How about waffles, or paninis?

$ – $ $

19. Airfare

Many airlines will let you pre-purchase flights or buy credits for airfare. If you want to empower a loved one to take a trip to someplace meaningful, consider this option.

$ $ $ $

20. Cinema-tastic!

Going to the movies isn't just a great distraction from grief, the two or three hours spent in the dark watching a major motion picture can also be moving and powerful. For years, when our kids were young, we didn't have the money to go to the movies. Then, a friend named Teresa mentioned a discount day at a movie theater near our home. That was such a gift to us, knowing that we could have a fun family outing to anticipate.

Maybe you can work with the manager at your local cinema. Tell him what you want to do. Maybe he will make you a good deal on tickets for your loved ones to visit the theater for a long time to come.

$ $

21. Now Streaming

What shows do you enjoy? Who do you enjoy them with? Can you purchase a box set of the show or a subscription to a streaming service so they can continue to enjoy them? Or maybe you already have a service, and you can make up a watch list of shows you'd love to see. Then, when your friends tune in, they will feel your presence with them.

Can you write a note telling them why you enjoy this show so much? Maybe you can even write questions you wonder about how the plot will unfold. Will Billy and Sally finally admit their love for one another? Will the vampires take over the city or will good overcome?

Then, when your friends or family watch this, they will sense your presence with them. (Especially when Billy and Sally finally find love).

Let's be honest for a moment, you might be sad that you won't get to watch these shows anymore. And that's okay. Feeling this way is not insignificant. It's normal.

Writing a few thoughts like this and securing the show for someone else can be an expression of your grief over missing future episodes.

FREE – $

22. Book Series

A good book can touch our hearts in special ways. Whether it's a non-fiction book that taught you valuable lessons, a regularly enjoyed children's book, or a work of fiction that moved you to tears, try to remember some of the most important books you have read.

Maybe you are in the middle of reading a series and you're pretty sure you won't be around to see all of them published. Talk with a friend who also enjoys the series, and share your thoughts about how it will end.

Purchase some books that meant a lot to you, and gift them to someone you think will enjoy them. When they do, they will feel connected to you–like you are right there with them.

$

23. Get Sporty

Few things bring people together like sports. Several members of my family are (American) football fans. We've been to games, watched games together, gone to other events like training camps, and generally cheered on a certain professional team and a university team. We've been in the stadium of the pro team dozens of times and on the campus of the university many times as well.

For us, those teams aren't just about winning or losing. They comprise a small part of our identity as a family: "We are Colts fans."

What could you purchase for someone who shares a rooting interest?

Go big. Pay for season tickets or autographed memorabilia. Or not-so-big. Buy a poster or light up decoration for the area where they watch the games at home.

Then, in a sense, you continue to root for that team alongside your fellow fans forever.

You can even have some fun with this.

One fan of another football team famously requested to have some of the players of his favorite team be pallbearers at his funeral. The team had been a perennial loser for many years–always coming up just short of winning a championship. So, the man said he wanted the players to carry his casket to his gravesite, so they could "let him down one last time."[6]

Ironically, six months later the team won their first championship. The inspiring part is that it brought this fan with the sense of humor back into the conversation after he had died, it gave him a sense of permanence.

$ – $ $ $ $

24. Get Sophisticated

Maybe sports aren't your thing, but theater or music is. How about changing out football season tickets for opera season tickets, or a sports poster for a memento from the gift shop at the local music hall or theater? Maybe you could pre-purchase concert tickets to your favorite band.

$ – $ $ $ $

25. Museum Passes

There are few better places for contemplation than a museum. If the museum has items from antiquity, it can give the visitor a sense of real longevity and permanence.

Perhaps your budget would allow you to purchase a pass for a special person—or even a membership.

$ $ $

26. Zoo Member

For years when our children were small, my in-laws gifted us passes to our local children's zoo. When money was tight (as it often was), we loved going to see the animals. The zoo became a part of our lives and an outlet when things were stressful.

Is there someone in your life that would think of you every time they use a zoo pass?

Don't forget to tell them your favorite animal so they can check in on that exhibit each time they visit.

$ $ $

27. Overload with Favorites

I have a brother-in-law who loves ketchup. The first time I had lunch with him, I thought he was trying to be funny. He poured out so much ketchup on his plate. However, he wasn't trying to be funny. He used it all!

When he got married, he received several large boxes of ketchup! It was a great laugh but also kind of sweet. It communicated–we noticed you are a little nuts about your favorite condiment. Instead of judging you as weird, let's help you indulge in ketchup.

What is a favorite of your loved one? A certain drink (soda, coffee, tea, wine)?[7] A certain snack? Type of pencil or pen? Make-up? Toiletry item?

If you know your loved one obsesses over having good floss, buy them enough floss to circle the globe.

It won't cost that much, you know they will probably actually use it. Plus, it communicates, "I noticed you are a little nuts about this, so, here you go!"

$

GET PRACTICAL

28. Membership Has its Benefits

Whether you are trying to find meaning in suffering or are just owning up to your mortality, consider purchasing a special person a membership to something meaningful to them.

Here's a short list of options to get you thinking:

- Local gym
- Shaving club

- Spa or massage therapy service

- Wholesale store

- Clothes delivery service

- Golf club

- Cheese of the month

- Coffee club

The key is to think of what will be meaningful to *them,* as well as you.

$ $ – $ $ $

29. Mow it Down

After a loved one dies, everything can change, even taking care of the yard. Maybe you are the one who has always mowed or found someone to mow.

When you are gone someday, it's not only going to be a hassle to find someone to care for the exterior of your residence, it's going to be one more reminder of your absence. However, if you can pay ahead for a lawn service to be performed after you are gone, the experience will be transformed into one of your presence–you continuing to care for the grass even after you are gone.

Better yet, like George in our case study, make this a two-for-one. Pick a special young person in your life and ask them if you can pay them to mow your grass for the next certain

137

number of years. Prepay for the first season and set the rest of the money aside with your loved one to bless this young person with a steady and meaningful job for the next several years.

$ $ – $ $ $

30. Maintenance Free Living

We already talked about the yard, but let's also consider a few other upcoming pieces of maintenance that you may have to manage around your home.

- What other annual tasks have been a headache in the past that you can help your loved one prepare for now?

- Who will open the pool in the backyard?

- Who will shovel the snow?

- Who will service the heating and air-conditioning?

- Who will clean the gutters next spring?

Taking care of some of the regular headaches for those close to you can make a big difference.

FREE – $ $ $

31. Regular Finances

In most families or partnerships, one person handles the bulk of the finances. Everyone else is a pain to this person because no one realizes what they do (thank you, Kristen!).

If you are the person who handles the finances, let me be honest with you. If you don't at least give *someone* some kind of heads up about your regular finances, the person you love most will end up with a major headache.

Some questions to consider:

- Do you need to share what money is where (checking, savings, retirement, investments, health savings accounts)?

- Even if they know *where* everything is, do they have access to it (Do they have the log-in IDs, passwords, cards, PINs, etc.?) Are they on the account as someone who can make decisions?

- Are they aware, at least generally, of your regular expenses; electric, gas, rent, etc.?

- Do they have access to the

computer where you have done most of the financial work? Access to and knowledge of appropriate files and/or spreadsheets? Do they have the right applications downloaded on their mobile device?

- Do they know who your insurance agent is and how to make contact with someone for your various types of insurance (home, life, auto, etc.)?

- Is their name on your most significant possessions and accounts (home, mortgage, automobiles, retirement, etc.)?

You might think they know all this, or could figure it out. However, a little forethought on your part will certainly help them.

FREE

32. Taxes and Death

A friend's cousin was dying, but he still had his wits very much about him. He was concerned for his spouse because he had always handled the taxes. So, a week or so before he died, he asked her to bring all the forms to the facility where he was receiving care. He went over them with her until he felt that she could handle the taxes in the future. I am not sure if this action meant more to her (knowing she would have some knowledge of how to do this in the future), or to him (feeling less anxious about the future tax seasons for his wife).

A few additional questions to consider about taxes:

- Do your loved ones know how you have done taxes in the past (done them yourself or utilized a tax preparer)?

- Do they know where the tax information and forms from past years are located?

- Do they know what receipts are important to save for your particular tax situation (housing, debt repayment, donations)?

- Do they know your method of paying taxes (payroll deduction, quarterly payments, etc.)?

Taxes are never fun, but when they are due during a season of grief, their complications can often increase.

FREE

33. House Cleaning

I once told Kristen that if I had extra money I would hire someone to clean our house every so often. I thought I was being considerate. Kristen didn't hear it that way.

However, providing for the house cleaning through a service or a friend you hire could be powerful for the people in your household who will remain after your death. Maybe, this service would be meaningful, even now, if you are sick and have lots of medical appointments and other activities that take your time more than they used to.

One word of caution. Make sure when you select a service or a friend that they are trustworthy (remember, they will be regularly entering the home of a grieving person or family), and bonded and insured. Not much would be worse than a family struggling with grief being taken advantage of or there being an accident and no insurance to cover it.

$ $ $

34. Car Service

Car repairs can be a headache for anyone, but many larger repair shops now have plans you can purchase. The plans can allow the automobile owner certain regularly scheduled maintenance (the most important part) and even discounts on repairs when needed.

Make sure you give all the documentation to your loved one who will own the car, and be sure to pick a reputable repair shop. And, if you like it to shine, be sure to also include car washes.

$ $ $

+++

Remember George and Mary? George had some simple gifts to provide. The truth is, even though it was a little expensive for George to pay Andre for two summers of mowing, Denny for years of car service, and the tax-preparer for her professional work, Mary would have had to pay most of that eventually, anyhow.

However, since George took the time to think through some gifts to provide, he added so much more weight and permanence to his relationship with Mary (even if she did like to yell at his picture once in a while).

Whether, like George, you give practical gifts or something more touching and sentimental, giving the gift doesn't just provide meaning for the one who receives it, it gives you a sense of meaning as well.

+++

We've come to the end of our list of 101 Ways to Find Meaning in Suffering. We've considered *words to express, actions to take,* and *gifts to provide.*

I hope you take a moment now to consider this last third of the list–*gifts to provide*–and choose one gift from the list that you can provide.

Let's keep talking. Go to PatrickRiecke.com to join a course, email me, or book me to speak to your group.

Before we conclude our conversation, I need to tell you a secret. Perhaps you have already realized the truth in the next couple of pages.

Notes

1. Psalm 50:10
2. Psalm 116:15
3. The scale ranges from one dollar sign ($) to four with one dollar sign indicating a small amount of money, and four indicating a large amount.
4. Be sure to check out *No Matter How Small: Understanding Miscarriage and Stillbirth*
5. https://www.parkview.com/community/dashboard/a-classic-game-gives-pediatric-patients-a-place-to-play
6. http://insider.foxnews.com/2017/08/25/philadelphia-eagles-fan-

wanted-players-pallbearers-jeffrey-clayton-riegel-funny-obituary

7. There's a sweet story about this in the book I co-authored with my wife, Kristen, *No Matter How Small: Understanding Miscarriage and Stillbirth*

Find Meaning Every Day

We seek meaning not only in the suffering life but in *life*.

Before we conclude, let me tell you a secret I realized halfway through the writing of this book. Perhaps you have had the same realization.

You don't have to be suffering to express words, take action, or provide gifts that will help you find meaning.

Yes, suffering often makes us more receptive to the importance of these words, actions, and gifts, but suffering is not required to make a purposeful attempt to find meaning.

Look at your life now. Consider it carefully; as though you have brought it all out onto the lawn, and are looking it over, one facet at a time.

What aspects of a life like yours would you consider meaningful?

What has *weight?*

What gives you a sense that it will last beyond your lifetime? What has real *permanence?*

Do you care for people at work?

Do you tend a garden?

Do you love an aging parent?

Again, this process is not usually about *making* meaning but more often about *finding* the meaning that already exists and leaning into it.

The point of this book has not been to provide an exhaustive list of ways that one can find meaning in suffering. The main goal has been to help you think about how *you* could find meaning in *your*

> **Life is not primarily a quest for pleasure... or a quest for power... but a quest for meaning.**[1]

life. Meaning in suffering, yes, but also meaning in every day.

If you found this book helpful, would you take a minute to leave an honest review online? That helps others to find this book and find meaning in their lives as well. If you are reading on a digital device, simply click here: Amazon Review. If you reading the print version, go to Amazon and search "Patrick Riecke" and leave a review. Thank you! You are helping me fulfill my goal of sharing this inspiration with the whole world.

Notes

1. Frankl, X

The Master of Meaning and Suffering

As a Christian, I cannot think about the dual topics suffering and meaning without thinking of Jesus.

He knew his end was coming and had been talking about it for some time.

His friends, much like well-meaning friends might today, his friends tried to stifle the "I'm dying" talk.

It's hard to know for sure how much information he was working with about when and how he would die, or when he accepted that death was coming.

To be honest, I think Jesus' life probably followed the Phase One through Phase Three model.

When he was a boy, I am sure there was a lot of conversation about the *plans* God had for him. After all, when people in your life believe you are born of a virgin and heralded by angels, expectations tend to increase.

Then, as Jesus's life went on, he faced plenty of hard times. It seems Joseph, his earthly father, probably died before Jesus reached adulthood. His goals were regularly opposed and stunted in a variety of ways, just like our goals often are. I am sure he prayed that God would help him overcome these hard times, a very Phase Two response.

Eventually, though, the picture became clear for Jesus. He was destined to die. I hate to tell you this, but you and I are destined to die as well.

Near the end of his life, Jesus began to regularly tell his friends that he was going to die.[1] He was in Phase Three and reminds us of our case studies of Bethany, Robert, and George. Like them, Jesus sought to find meaning in Phase Three. Phase Three is often a small window of time–smaller than we wish it was. This was also true for Jesus.

It could be argued that his window was just one night. That night is recorded beautifully in the Gospel of John.

GLORY AND ETERNAL LIFE

On the verge of his death, in Phase Three, Jesus began by praying for himself, expressing words as a way to find meaning.

His prayer centered on two topics, and they are going to sound *very* familiar.

First, he used the word 'glory' five times in his prayer. Glory means weight and significance. The Greek word is *doxe,* which means to bring honor to. It's where we get the word 'doxology'. The Hebrew word for glory is *kavod,* which means "weight".

Second, he uses the word for 'eternal life' twice. In Greek, this is one word–*ionios,* which means an experience with no beginning and no end. It always is.

Weight and permanence. Glory and eternal life.

Jesus, facing his death, prayed about glory–weight, and eternal life–permanence.

FRIENDS

Next, Jesus prays about the people in his life. He begins by praying about the truth that has been revealed to his followers–gifts he had provided for them.

Then he prayed a very interesting sentence that could be the subtitle of this book.

"I am coming to you now [I am dying], but I say these things while I am still in the world, so that my friends may have the full measure of my joy within them."[2]

"I am dying, and I realize that I cannot change that," Jesus said.

"However, as I face my mortality, my imminent death, I am saying things while I am still here. Since I am not dead yet, let me take full advantage of the time I have left to get some things done. The reason is so that those who love me will be filled with joy. And not just any joy, *my* joy. I want them to experience joy internally that is distinctly connected to me in some way." Remember, meaning is always concrete and specific.

Jesus, as he faced his death, said, in effect, "I know I am going to die. Now what I want is for those close to me to find meaning, glory (weight), and eternal life (permanence), so that I can leave this world feeling as though I have given them a joyful part of who I am."

In this, Jesus is our model. The joy that he gave them, the meaning he helped them find in the midst of suffering, reverberates some two millennia later.

Notes

1. Matthew 16:21ff
2. John 17:3

Appendix A--A Note to Professionals

Upon first looking over the contents of this book, a fellow author and chaplain concluded, "We need a note to us. A note to people who do this, at least in part, for a living."

If you are a clergy person, social worker, support group leader, hospice worker, counselor, nurse or physician, medical tech, or anyone who helps people in Phase Three with regularity, these next few words are for you.

HELPING OTHERS FIND MEANING

There are windows of opportunity to help others do the work I have described in this book:

- After a chronic or terminal diagnosis has been given.

- When patients, parishioners, or clients have an existential crisis.

- When they accept a move into Phase Three.

- As a follow up to an Advance Care Planning conversation.

Here's my not-so-secret hope.

I hope that you will use this list as a way to help others find meaning, as well as yourself. A counselor could keep this book on her shelf and pull it out whenever she sensed one of these windows of opportunity. A social worker with hospice could keep it close by to talk through with families. A pastor could have it for times when he is visiting the sick in the hospital.

CARE FOR YOURSELF

Doing what you do is difficult. It's soul-wrenching at times, and it takes a toll.

The group U2 surprised me with these words in their song "The Troubles". Maybe you can understand the experience they describe.

> Somebody stepped inside your soul.
> Somebody stepped inside your soul.
> Little by little they robbed and stole.
> Till somebody else was in control.
> God knows it's not easy.
> I'm taking on the shape of
> Someone else's pain.

In chapter three, I described supporting a family whose toddler died suddenly and unexpectedly. That family stepped inside my soul. For the next few days, I wasn't myself. A couple of days later, I found myself standing in my backyard, just staring.

I admitted that I needed a little self-care. I needed to be revitalized--to find a way to reinject life into my soul.

If I don't care for myself, my soul, who will? If you don't care for yourself, who will?

You have to find those activities that will reinflate your soul after bearing another person's great pain. After you hold the hand of a dying person or counsel the widow in her grief, you have to go play tennis, or watch your favorite comedy, ride your bike, or go out with friends.

Your boss can't do this for you. Your patients, clients, or parishioners can't do it for you, either.

Neglecting self-care isn't noble. Or selfless. Giving everything and getting nothing isn't caring.

It's foolish.

It's short-sighted.

And it *will* ruin you and your impact in whatever sphere you work.

It's a hero-complex that we aren't meant to hold.

Musician Avicci writes, "I tried carrying the weight of the world. But I only have two hands."

The best way for chaplains in our department to do the very best work for our patients is to take time away. To take vacations. To admit it when they are at their breaking point. To get counseling. To do the things that rejuvenate them whether it's taking a trip or doing puzzles at home.

Me?

I write books like this to you.

I date my wife.

And I watch videos that make me laugh.

I read and don't talk to anyone for a few hours.

I walk.

I go to my favorite wholesale store and usually don't buy a thing.

No one else will do this for me.

But when I do this, I fill my heart with all sorts of treasures that I can then pour out into the lives of those around me.

If I can serve you in any way, by speaking to your group or just you personally, find me at PatrickRiecke.com.

Appendix B--Advance Care Planning

ED'S STORY

Ed is a very elderly man whose family you have known for a long time. He has been sick for as long as you have known him, and you have visited him in the hospital many times.

He is well-loved by his large family.

Now, Ed is hospitalized again. He is in respiratory failure, his kidneys are shutting down, and he has a recently discovered inoperable cancer mass. He is unresponsive, not doing well at all. You happen to be in the room when the physician comes to visit.

She isn't very hopeful.

Ed, she tells the family, is at the end of his life.

You could tell that the tone of the family was negative before the doctor came in, but the situation escalates during the conversation.

As soon as the physician starts to sound like she's 'giving up', the tone of the family goes from tense to angry. When she uses the phrase "Do not resuscitate", the family abruptly ends the conversation and tells her to get out. Their reaction seems to not only close the door to the doctor, but to the entire idea that Ed might not overcome his current condition.

After the physician gracefully exits, the family turns to one another and you, and says things like, "Can you believe she wants us to pull the plug on grandpa? She must not have any faith. We know he will get better."

You look at the motionless Ed, who has tubes coming and going everywhere, including a large tube that is in his mouth, helping him breathe. You certainly want to be optimistic, but things don't look good.

A couple of days later you hear that Ed is still not getting any better, that the hospital still wants to take him off of his ventilator, but that Ed is still a full code[1] and is getting dialysis every few days.

Some questions that may arise from the family at this stage are listed below. Imagine the family asking you these questions.

Don't the doctors have any faith?

Shouldn't we do everything to save him?

Can't God heal him?

Shouldn't we at least keep him alive until Aunt Betty arrives from Arizona?

Should we look for an LTAC facility?[2]

Are we playing God if we take him off the vent?

ED'S WISHES: ADVANCE CARE PLANNING

There are other important questions for Ed. Questions that might take the focus off what the family wants or what the healthcare team thinks is best, and shine a light on what Ed's wishes might be–what he might find meaningful during his last days on earth.

Did Ed ever express his wishes if he found himself in this situation? Did he ever have an Advance Care Planning conversation? Does he have any advance directives completed?

What is an Advance Directive?

> Advance directive is a term that refers to your spoken and written instructions about your future medical care and treatment. By stating your healthcare choices in an advance directive, you help your family and physician understand your wishes about your medical care.[3]

159

If Ed completed an advance directive, it might answer questions such as:

1. What does he want to be done medically?

Advance Care Planning covers important questions. The conversation helps people consider (in advance) what medical interventions they might request or decline. This planning can answer questions about whether or not a patient would want to be on a ventilator for a long time or how they would feel about having a medical situation that limited their ability to interact with or understand the world around them.

2. How far does he want to take his healthcare?

In an Advance Care Planning conversation, Ed may have indicated a preference concerning CPR, or certain medicines, or procedures in certain situations. That would certainly help the conversation between his family and the healthcare team.

3. Does Ed want to be intubated for a long time? Does he want a feeding tube?

Unfortunately, Ed is very sick. The standard, generally, is to keep a patient intubated (the ventilator tube down their throat) for about two weeks. Since Ed isn't improving, the possibility of removing the ventilator means he might not survive. Did Ed ever indicate what he would want in this situation?

One of the most difficult conversations can center around the feeding tube. No one wants to think that they are starving their loved ones. But in some situations, a feeding tube may not be making the person better and could even be a burden to the patient (failed tubes, infection, digestive concerns).

4. Did Ed think about nursing facilities?

Opinions about being in a long term care facility (nursing home, assisted living, etc.) vary widely. Some people embrace it as their new community. Others would rather remain at home or in a hospital.[4] Advance Care Planning helps a person think through these decisions before they become urgent.

5. What matters most to Ed as his health declines?

This is the most important question—especially if we care about Ed finding meaning, even in this situation. Advance Care Planning facilitators are often trained to ask the question, "What does living well mean to you?" Or, "If you were having a good day, what would you be doing, what would be happening?" Answers vary from time spent with family, to going to work, to just being able to wake up and see the sunshine. You can see how this question, answered in advance, would have helped Ed.

6. Who does Ed want to make his decisions?

Of course, Ed would like to make his own decisions about his healthcare, but right now, he cannot. He has a lot of family members who may have a variety of opinions. But is there one person in Ed's life who has talked with him about healthcare wishes? Does that person have the courage to follow through on whatever his wishes may be even if they don't line up with her own desires? This designation of a health care representative, or health care agent, is not a difficult process. Our chaplains help patients complete these forms every day in our health system. They could have helped Ed complete one before he was quite so sick. If he hasn't done it by now, however, it may be too late.

7. Does Ed have any of this in writing?

This is the most practical question. Having a difficult conversation about all these questions is the starting point, but having advance directive documents makes healthcare decisions simpler.

A leading resource for having conversations that include such important questions is an organization called Respecting Choices®.[5] Also, your local, state, or federal government likely has some resources available.

Here are some basics for an advance directive form:

- The form must indicate the wishes of the patient.

- The form must be signed by the patient (meaning they must be able to understand what they are signing).

- The form must be signed by other witnesses or a

notary, as required by the form or applicable local statutes.

8. What is the best-case scenario if Ed continues to receive aggressive care?

Some people respond well to aggressive care. When people are young, otherwise healthy, strong, and have lots of support, it's more likely they will have a positive outcome even if their current health situation is really scary.

Although Ed has lots of support, he is not young, strong, or otherwise healthy. Even if every medical intervention works perfectly, in what shape will it leave Ed?

A related difficult question is "Is dialysis 'doing harm' if he is not going to recover?" Dialysis can be a painful and involved process. There are needle sticks, flushing of fluids, rotating of the patient, and repeated tests. Having a tube in your throat to help you breathe is no different. Many patients who recover after being intubated report jaw soreness, a sensitive throat, and a dry cough for some time.

9. How do you think Ed feels about his situation now?

Even the least responsive patient will occasionally wince in pain, or they might seem at peace. Perhaps they are communicating non-verbally; a squeeze of a hand or nodding of the head, tears in the eyes, or other means. Even though Ed can't say much, we can learn, upon careful observation, a lot about how he is feeling about the situation.

10. What will it look like if a Full Code is called for Ed?

A code is a violent event. Chest compressions, shock to the chest, artificial respiration, and loads of medication are no small experience. It's not like in the movies where after a few moments of chest compressions and the person revives, sits up, and thanks his rescuer.

In fact, according to the American Heart Association, the statistics for CPR after cardiac arrest are not promising, even if the patient is in the hospital already. [6] In 2016, for example, less than 25% of patients who received CPR while hospitalized survived until their discharge from the hospital. Other reports show even lower success rates.

While every situation is unique, it's clear that being coded (receiving full interventional care if you lose your pulse) while in the hospital is not a good sign for your survival.

Ed has multiple co-morbidities (diseases or illnesses that could cost him his life). He has respiratory failure (which is why he is on a breathing machine), his kidneys are shutting down, and he has significant cancer for which there is no real treatment.

If Ed has CPR, what are the chances that he will be the one in four who survives until he is discharged from the hospital?

But Ed's family insists that he will get better. They don't trust the hospital or anyone who tells them otherwise. Ed's family is waiting for a miracle.

+++

Advance Care Planning is important. Some people want everything done in every situation but many do not. My wife and I recently had an Advance Care Planning conversation, even though we are both healthy and young. Without revealing all of our wishes, I can confidently say that neither of us would want to be in Ed's situation. Let me be more specific. If I were in Ed's situation, Kristen would know that I would not view this as a meaningful situation in which I would want her to keep me on the ventilator and going to dialysis. She would, after a careful conversation with the care team, elect to remove the interventions.

If you would like to have an Advance Care Planning conversation, contact your physician, local hospital, or look for the appropriate documents on your local government website. For other introductions, simply search Advance Care Planning.

+++

You visit Ed in the hospital again a few days later. Only a few family members are at his bedside as the early morning sunlight shoots through the room. The beams of light contrast with the dark sadness of the family, and the clinical beeping of machines that hovers over Ed.

Ed is stuck.

He did not do any Advance Care Planning. He has no advance directives completed. In fact, it seems he never said much about what he would want to be done in a situation like this, and it seems no one asked.

Now his condition is static—the machines are keeping him from dying, but they aren't making him better. His family continues their "do everything and wait for a miracle" approach.[7] Likely, because of this, the family and the care team are no longer enjoying good communication. Every time Ed's nurse comes in, she seems tense and defensive, and the family is dismissive of her. You get the feeling that the doctors have been avoiding Ed's room when the family is visiting. When there is a breakdown between the patient, family, and healthcare team, there are no winners.

At first, Ed's family resisted allowing him to die so Aunt Betty could come from Arizona. Then, they wanted him to be moved to a long term facility where he could remain intubated. All the while, Ed was getting dialysis, remained a full code, and was slowly going downhill.

+++

On day 17 of Ed's hospitalization, at eleven-thirty at night, his heart failed. A code was called and CPR performed, according to the family's wishes.

Ed, an elderly and frail man, received chest compressions, shock to his chest, and extreme medications.

Only three members of Ed's large family were visiting when the Code Blue was called—Ed's youngest daughter and her two children. His 17-year-old granddaughter, Tanisha, and his 14-year-old grandson, Brian, watched as a team of more than a dozen clinicians went to work on their papaw.

Ed died after being coded for 47 traumatic minutes.

Forty-seven minutes.

His frail body nearly broke under CPR, all because his family got stuck in Phase Two.

All the tubes coming in and out of his body were askew, and he seemed to be in agony as he died in front of Brian and Tanisha.

When we are willing to wade into Phase Three, beautiful things happen. People like George provide gifts. People like Bethany express words. People like Robert take action.

But when we try to stay in Phase One or Phase Two, we can miss the meaning that's possible in suffering. Ed's family missed a chance to find meaning in his suffering.

+++

What if Ed's family could have entered Phase Three?

Maybe they would have stood around his bed, sharing their favorite stories of their father and grandfather. Maybe Brian, his youngest grandchild, would have learned that his grandfather always wanted to be a poet and that he had a box full of poetry at home. And maybe, just maybe, Brian would have taken those poems, typed them up, and put them in a book. Maybe Brian would have followed in his footsteps and done some co-writing with his grandpa's archived poems later in life, and published their work together. Instead, what did Brian get in the last moments of his grandpa's life?

A traumatic image of death, a distrust of healthcare, and maybe a loss of faith in God.

Since Brian was the only one in the family who would have been inclined to do all this with the poetry, and since the family never waded into Phase Three, Brian had no idea his grandpa was a poet—writing many of his works while he was a ruddy young man in the Army. Those possibilities disappeared like a vapor of things that could have been.

That's why it's so important, when it's time, to wade with people into Phase Three and help them find meaning in suffering.

We've paused to remember Phase Three and to emphasize the importance of Advance Care Planning specifically because it helps create space for finding meaning.

If meaning is the contents we are looking for, Advance Care Planning and wading into Phase Three build the container for those contents. We build a box which we can fill with meaning when we are willing to have frank and honest conversations about the fact that none of us live forever. We build the box by considering the medical and relational questions that are included in Advance Care Planning.

Before we can find meaning, we have to create this space in which we are willing to seek meaning.

We have to ask Bethany what she wants to do.

Robert has to make his list of important places.

George has to ring the doorbell at Andre's house.

If you are the type of person who would read a book like this, it's an honor to tell you a secret. You are the person in your circle of friends or family who needs to introduce this type of conversation. If you are willing to read a book like this (especially all the way to the end), you will bring up difficult conversations like this.

Most people won't, so it's good that you will. To continue this conversation, take my online course at PatrickRiecke.com/courses.

Notes

1. Meaning that if his heart stops, he will have CPR and other interventions to bring his heartbeat back.

2. Long Term Acute Care Facility. These facilities can take care of patients like Ed for a longer time than hospitals.

3. https://www.in.gov/isdh/25880.htm

4. See #24 in Chapter 7

5. https://respectingchoices.org/

6. http://cpr.heart.org/AHAECC/CPRAndECC/General/UCM_477263_Cardiac-Arrest-Statistics.jsp

7. For a discussion on waiting for miracles, see my first book, How to Talk with Sick, Dying, and Grieving People

More Resources

Make an Impact on Your Group: Schedule a Live Presentation!

Have you enjoyed this book? Do you know of a group that would benefit from a presentation of this content? Go to PatrickRiecke.com and book Patrick Riecke to speak to your group today! Picture the concepts, education, and stories in this book, a life-changing conversation, and your group, better equipped than ever, to care for people in crisis. To schedule a keynote message, workshop or event go PatrickRiecke.com now.

E-Mail Newsletter

While you are on the website, for more free content, videos, and advice on helping people who are sick, dying, or grieving, sign up for Patrick's free newsletter! When you sign up, you will receive access to the five helpsheets in the back of this book, and several video trainings where Patrick explains how to do what we have talked about in this book. Visit PatrickRiecke.com now to sign up.

Purchase the Other Books in the Series

If you liked this book, you might benefit from the rest of the series:

How to Talk with Sick, Dying, and Grieving People: When There are No Magic Words to Say by Patrick Riecke

No Matter How Small: Understanding Miscarriage and Stillbirth by Patrick and Kristen Riecke

Giving a Life Meaning: How to Lead Funerals, Memorial Services, and Celebrations of Life by Dr. Jon Swanson.

Wallet Cards for Hospital Visits

You never know when you will end visiting a hospital. So, be prepared with a FREE wallet card telling you what to ALWAYS, SOMETIMES, and NEVER do when you visit a hospital. Claim your wallet card today at PatrickRiecke.com/Resources.

Online Video Course

Take your understanding to the next level by signing up for my online video course today. Not only will you have access to video teaching based on this book, but you'll also learn:

- How to select a funeral home

- How to talk with children about death

- The difference between pain medication and assisted suicide

- How to perform advance care planning and find meaning in life

To begin my online video on demand course today, go to PatrickRiecke.com/courses.

About the Author

Rev. Patrick Riecke, M.A., is the Director of Chaplaincy and Volunteers and Chairperson for the Ethics Committee at Parkview Health. With over 20 years of ministry experience both in churches and in healthcare, Riecke is also an engaging speaker and is available for a small number of speaking engagements each year. He draws not only on his own experience but also the daily ministry experience of other chaplains and friends. He holds a B.A. in Bible and Preaching from Johnson University and an M.A. in New Testament from Cincinnati Bible Seminary, with awards for scholarship and church ministry. Riecke lives in Fort Wayne, IN, with his wife, four children and enjoys having breakfast on his back deck overlooking their neighborhood pond.

For more content, social media links, to join his mailing list, or to book Patrick for an event, go to www.PatrickRiecke.com.